D1000515

GENESIS & COMMON SENSE

GENESIS & COMMON SENSE

The Reality: Creation vs. Evolution

ENESIS & COMMON SENSE

The Reality: Creation vs. Evolution

Clarence Schreur

Ralph Tanner Associates, Inc.
BOOK PUBLISHERS
Prescott, Arizona

This Book
is
Dedicated to
My wife Evelyn
Without whose patience
Understanding and cooperation
This book would not have been
made possible

Contents

Acknowledgements

My interest in the sciences, and Christianity, began many years ago and, of course, I am grateful to the family environment for encouraging those interests . . . I am also grateful for the personal freedom we enjoy in the United States of America which enables us to pursue those interests.

Perhaps, too, this is the opportunity to express my sincere appreciation to the many persons who gave of their time and knowledge during the formative years and who exerted such a positive influence during those relationships.

In the preparation of the manuscript there were many friends who shared their expertise and gave their time; since space limitations prohibits me from mentioning all by name, I would like to thank James Beasley and H. McCormick Lintz for lending their personal support. And, especially, I want to thank Ralph Tanner and his associates, Barbara Brook and Carol Scotti, for the professional skills they shared with me in the publication of this book.

March, 1983
Clarence Schreur
Prescott, Arizona

PREFACE

The controversy between Religion and Science has been going on for many decades, but in recent years this has blossomed into a full-fledged verbal war. Television-sponsored debates, magazine articles, and newspaper coverage have brought the focus of attention on the subject of Creation vs. Evolution, even to the extent of legal battles and court decisions with regard to the right to teach or not to teach both subjects in the public schools.

The purpose of this book is not to take issue with one side against the other, but rather to examine the basic claims and theories of both sides and to determine as far as possible where the truth lies.

One thing that is very evident is the fact that the dogmatic, unsupported position taken by certain religious organizations has caused untold millions of individuals to look with disdain and contempt on religion in general.

On the other hand, Christians in particular reject in toto the theory of Evolution as it is commonly taught today. Since there can be but one truth, it follows that one opponent in the great debate must be right and the other wrong. However, since there are numerous divisions and details involved in the controversy, it is possible that neither party is completely right or completely wrong.

Since the controversy is primarily concerned with the teachings of the Holy Bible, and the book of Genesis in particular, it is of utmost importance to be sure that our interpretation of Scripture is in complete agreement with the original writings. In other words, that the translation is accurate and portrays the exact meaning given in the language in which the Scripture was written, in this case the Hebrew or Aramaic language.

It is also mandatory that Scripture be compared with Scripture in order to assure the student that the translation and interpretation are harmonious, without conflict. If there is disagreement, then either our interpretation or understanding is in error.

Just as the foregoing applies to the religious side of the argument, the same rules apply to the Scientific viewpoint. Well known is the fact that Scientific theories are frequently changed as new discoveries disclose the fallacies of such theories. Nevertheless, there are some things which are obvious or so well documented that they must be accepted as truth.

With the foregoing in mind, I have attempted to set the record straight both as to certain Biblical truths as well as certain Scientific theories. Obviously, I will be criticized by both sides, and will be bombarded with counterarguments. However, if this book leads both sides to at least consider the alternatives, it will have served its purpose.

Clarence Schreur
Prescott, Arizona

CHAPTER I

In The Beginning

he sun was just about to disappear behind the low hills covered with pine, juniper, and oak, when the delivery boy tossed the evening paper in the general direction of Rev. Clyde Spangler's house. Normally the paper would have landed in the bushes bordering the front porch, or else ended up in the rain gutter, but for some unexplainable reason it landed right in the middle of the flagstone walk leading from the street to the front door of the Reverend's modest home.

Reverend Spangler had been sitting in his favorite rocking chair on the small front porch when this took place, and at once got up and walked out to retrieve the paper. Picking it up he walked slowly back to the porch, glancing over the headlines as he did so. Besides the usual bold headlines reporting on the lack of progress in the Middle East talks, and new investigations of corrupt government officials, one lesser headline seemed to stand out sharply: "Missing Link Believed Found."

The Reverend was a devout man, and by theologic standards very fundamental. Yet, he was not narrow in his views, and

1

always studied every new interpretation or idea that might shed light on difficult passages or portions of Scripture. He was well aware of the fact that very diverse positions were held by even the most learned and sincere theologians on many Bibical matters such as the days of creation, or the extent of the flood. However, the thought that the very basic tenants of the faith might be shaken by actually finding the so-called missing link, thus confirming the arguments of the Evolutionists, was almost too much for him. Shakily he sat down in his chair and began to read the article. As he did, he realized how unfounded his fears had been, for as in so many previous articles, it turned out that the fossils that had been found, and labeled "missing link," were once again only fragments of a man-like creature, although admittedly, more complete and more nearly human than most of the other great finds.

The good Reverend had barely finished reading the article when the telephone rang. Mrs. Spangler answered it and called her husband to the phone. "It's one of the Deacons from the church, Jim Martin," Mrs. Spangler said. The Reverend got up from his chair and walked briskly into the house. "Hello, Jim. What can I do for you," he asked. "Pastor, have you seen the evening paper? There's an article telling about finding the missing link, right on the front page" the voice on the phone replied. "Yes, I just now finished reading it" the Reverend said. "Why?" "Well, every Pastor under whom I have sat, including yourself, has held to the story of creation. Doesn't this prove that the Evolutionists were right all along?" Jim's voice was almost accusatory, and he appeared to be very shaken by this latest article on the missing link. Without waiting for a reply, Jim continued. "Do you suppose we could get together some evening this week and sit down to discuss this? I'm really quite upset, and I'd like to get it straight if possible." "Well, let me look at my calendar. I think Friday night is open." There was a short pause and the Reverend Spangler said, "Yes, Friday would be O.K. Why don't you come over about 7:00 o'clock." "Thanks, Pastor," Jim said. "I'll be there."

Reverend Spangler's doorbell sounded promptly at 7:00 o'clock. Opening the door, he found Jim Martin standing there, and with him another man whom the Reverend didn't recognize. "Hello Pastor," Jim said. "This is a friend of mine, Harry Bolin. He and I have been discussing this matter of Evolution, and he asked if he might come along with me tonight. I hope you don't mind," he added almost hesitantly. "Not at all," the Reverend said. "Very glad to meet you Mr. Bolin. Please come in."

It was immediately obvious that Jim was not interested in idle chit-chat, but wanted to get started on the subject at hand. So, after the usual questions about Jim's wife and family, Reverend Spangler said, "Since I talked with you yesterday, Jim, I have been giving a great deal of thought to this whole matter. I don't think we can arrive at any satisfactory answer to the controversy between the Creationists and Evolutionists without starting at the very beginning. As you know, the only written record we have that has any real bearing on this subject is the book of Genesis." And with this introduction, the Reverend began a discourse on the entire subject of Creation, and the events that followed as given in the book of Genesis, and referred to in other portions of Scripture.

"Before we look at the Scriptural account," Reverend Spangler said, "we must realize that this was written some 3500 years ago. Many of the events recorded in this book were familiar to the Hebrews, having been passed down from generation to generation by word of mouth. It was not necessary for Moses to go into details in many cases for this reason. Likewise, the details are also missing from the creation account, no doubt partly due to the fact that the Hebrews took it for granted that God had created everything. They did not need detailed evidence or arguments to convince them of this. In fact, only within the last several hundred years has there been any serious doubts as to this truth. Even so called Pagan religions for the most part accept the idea of creation by a Supreme Being without question. The same may be said for the story of the flood. Many primitive peoples scattered over the face of the earth have legends of a great flood, and accept it as fact. But let's start with Genesis Chapter 1 and Verse 1, and discuss that as we go."

The good Reverend didn't realize at the time that this discussion was to continue for many, many sessions over a period of several months. Nor did he realize the amount of study and research that was to go into these discussions. And little did he realize the implications and conclusions that would result from this study.

" 'In the beginning'," read Reverend Spangler. "We start right off with such a profound statement that we realize from the very first words of the Book that this must have indeed been Divinely inspired. Certainly Moses had no idea of when the beginning was, and as far as he or the Hebrews were concerned it didn't matter. The important thing was that there had been a beginning. At this very point the Evolutionists for the most part disagree with Creationists." At this point, Jim spoke up. "Just what is the definition of these two groups?" he asked. "Evolutionists," the Reverend replied, "generally hold to the theory that life on this planet was started by a spontaneous act, and that this evolved, changed and mutated to produce every known form of life. They base this theory on the observed adaptations which many forms of life have made to their environment, and on the similarity between many existing and fossil forms of life. The Creationists on the other hand, believe and hold to the Scriptural account given in Genesis which records that God created all forms of life, both vegetable and animal. There are of course, many intermediate theories and beliefs such as those who believe in an initial Creation followed by evolution to produce all the life forms that have and do exist."

At this point Harry Bolin spoke up. "Reverend, I am a scientist. My specialty is organic chemistry, but I have also studied a great deal in geology, paleontology, and astronomy. I believe in God, but I find it very difficult to accept the story of creation as it is usually presented. I find it especially hard to accept the theory that our entire universe and everything it contains was created in seven days."

"Well, we are getting ahead of ourselves a little now," the Reverend said. "We'll come to that in due time, but you should know that many of the most respected Bible scholars do not accept the seven literal twenty-four hour days of creation. I think I can show you from Scripture where this doctrine originated and some of the opposing arguments. But let's go back to the beginning."

4

CHAPTER II

Moses and Religion

he Book of Genesis is one of five books credited to Moses in the Holy Bible. While there are those who believe these were actually written at a much later date than during Moses' lifetime, it is generally believed that he was in fact the author of these writings. No doubt they were set down on papyrus by a scribe, or scribes acting under Moses direction. There are a number of names and incidents recorded in these books which would not have been known at a later date as they were lost to the knowledge of man, in some cases until our own generation.

"A case in point is the account given in Exodus Chapter 5 where Pharaoh gives the order to withhold straw from the Israelites for use in making bricks. For many centuries it was thought that the use of straw in making bricks was for strengthening the bricks through the fibrous nature of the straw. Not known until around the turn of this century was the fact that this is not the purpose of straw in brick making. When straw is soaked in water, a substance known as gallotannic acid leaches out, which has the property of making clay much easier to work.

"Archeological research during the nineteenth and twentieth centuries have shown that some bricks made in Egypt during the period covered by the Exodus account were in fact made without straw, while others contained straw.

"Further support to the belief that Moses was the author of the Pentateuch is literary style. Every writer has a style which reflects his personality, beliefs, education, and experiences. This is brought out very pointedly in a comparison of the four Gospels, where four different individuals, writing about the same person, present a completely different view, yet, completely harmonious with that of one another.

"Moses was without doubt a well educated, brilliant man. He was reared in Pharaoh's own household, and also received the best formal training available in that day. Despite this, he was not an outgoing person, and apparently not adept at public speaking. He hated oppression, and demanded complete honesty and accuracy in all his dealings with others.

"Through the wise intervention of Moses' older sister, the daughter of Pharaoh was persuaded to employ Moses' own mother to nurse the baby and care for him until he was old enough to turn him over to Pharaoh's daughter as her own son. During these formative years, Moses' mother without doubt taught him about her God and the heritage of the Israelites. He certainly would not have acquired this from the teachings of the Egyptians.

"Bible critics have suggested that the writings of Moses had their genesis in the traditions and writings available in the libraries of Egypt, which certainly contained accounts and stories of other peoples commonly known to the Egyptians. They had trade with many other countries, near and far, and had engaged in conflict with other countries as well, taking prisoners, who would no doubt have related traditions and accounts to their Egyptian captors, some of which have very likely been handed down from father to son for many generations.

"The similarity between the Genesis account of the flood, and the Babylonian account found on clay tablets in excavations at Ninevah, has been used as proof that Moses simply repeated what he had learned from tradition. However, a close comparison of the two accounts show a vast difference in the basis for the flood, as well as many other details. There are in fact traditions of a great flood to be found in many diverse civilizations around the world, attesting to the fact that there was such an event. We will consider this in greater detail later in our discussions.

"If Moses was the educated, intelligent person I believe he was, and if a writer discloses his character in his writings, then we would expect these qualities to be evident throughout the account given in the Pentateuch. That is to say, we should expect the account to be accurate, concise, and truthful. However, we should also expect that the language used would be geared to the intellect of that day. If this is the case, let us consider for a moment the opening words of the first book of the Bible. 'In the beginning God created the heavens and the earth.' This statement is so simple, yet, so completely overwhelming and grand as to defy comment, yet, completely satisfied the purpose Moses had in mind and set forth the Supreme Being as the Creator of all things. Now suppose that Moses had written something like this. 'Fifteen billion years ago, all the stars and planets were concentrated in one spot in the vastness of space. A tremendous nuclear explosion took place, scattering the matter in every direction, and gradually the particles were drawn together into clouds which gradually cooled to become stars and planets.'

"An obvious fact is that the people of that day would not have understood what Moses was talking about, and would very likely have stoned him to death or at least considered him completely demented. Instead, the first sentence in the book of Genesis has become the cornerstone of faith in God and the basis for belief in creation as opposed to Materialism, in whatever form.

"Unfortunately, because the book of Genesis is written in such simple language, it has become very easy to interpret it in many different ways. There are those who take an extremely dogmatic view of the book, especially the first chapter, as it relates to the *days* of creation. In contrast, there are those who consider the account to be completely figurative, and not to be taken literally in any sense.

"Intensely interesting is the fact that every major civilization that has ever existed has centered around religion. The great cities of the past whose ruins have been examined by archeologists, have revealed that religion was the core of their way of life. Temples, altars, tombs, all bear witness to the fact that worship, sacrifice and dedication consumed much of their effort, time and worldly goods. Even small tribes in isolated parts of the earth apparently have had some form of religion, whether simply superstition or a more sophisticated practice. This is true even today as missionaries or explorers go into the remote areas of the world.

"Atheistic critics of the Bible explain this universal need for religion as a result of a need to explain natural phenomena, such as eclipses, lightning, thunder, volcanism, and other natural phenomenon.

"Moses believed, practiced and wrote that there is a living, Supreme Being Who calls Himself 'I AM,' and Who is called 'God' or 'Jehovah': Moses ascribes the creation to this One, and particularly in the book of Genesis, also ascribes to Him the miraculous escape from Egypt and the preservation of the Israelites in the great Sinai desert for forty years.

"How much more logical to recognize in the perverted religious systems that have dominated civilizations throughout history and pre-history a degenerate form of true worship of a living God. Assuming that Adam and Eve did in fact have an intimate relationship with God, as related by Moses in the opening chapters of Genesis, would it not be natural for mankind to gradually alter and pervert this knowledge as it was passed from father to son down through the ages? The introduction of idols and images, as well as the substitution of animals, planets and the sun and moon for an invisible, spirit God should not be surprising since this is still common practice today.

"Fundamental Christianity is based on the belief in the verbal inspiration of the Scriptures. That is, that the original writings were without error and were written by men who were so yielded to the direction of the Holy Spirit that they used just the right words to convey the message that God had for mankind. Students of the Scriptures are amazed over and over again by

8

evidence of such inspiration. This is especially true of the New Testament which was written in Greek which has many more shades of meaning than our English language. The choice of words is extremely important in many cases to convey a particular thought, which could easily be misunderstood if a word with slightly different meaning was used. For this reason great effort has gone into the new translations of the Bible; that is, to bring out in our modern English language what was so clearly expressed in the original.

"Likewise, there are changes in meaning of words with time even within a particular language. Words which had a specific meaning in 1611 when the King James translation was made available, in many cases have an entirely different meaning now. A case in point is the word translated "peculiar" in reference to Christians who are called a peculiar people. Today, that word conjures up the thought of someone slightly crazy, or at least an irrational person. In the original it meant unusual, remarkable, or set apart.

"Although the newer translations of Scripture have helped a great deal in bringing us a better understanding and knowledge of the Bible, there are still some areas, particularly in the book of Genesis, which are not only difficult to understand and therefore the subject of controversy, but which do not seem to fit in with certain geologic, astronomic, and archeologic findings and theories. This is especially true if a dogmatic position is taken on certain portions of Scripture for which traditional interpretations continue to be considered the true and only possible one.

"When Moses wrote the Pentateuch, his purpose was not to write a detailed account of all that had taken place on the earth since the day of creation. His purpose was to lay a ground work for the choice of Israel as God's chosen people, and then to record the various events and experiences of the Israelites from their captivity in Egypt to the arrival at Caanan after forty years in the desert.

"Few problems arise from a study of the experiences of the Jews after leaving Egypt, although critics question the validity of the Red Sea crossing, the giving of the tablets of the Law, the capture of Jerico, and other miraculous events. However, it is an historical fact that the Jews did indeed leave Egypt, wander for forty years in the desert, and finally conquer Caanan. It would be extremely difficult, if not impossible, to believe that the events recorded by Moses could possibly have taken place without Divine intervention.

"It might be very difficult to refute some of the critics of the Bible were it not for one extremely important event in history. I refer to the birth of Jesus Christ. Jesus Himself verified a number of the events recorded by Moses, and also placed Moses in a position of credibility and even reverence. Someone has said that Jesus Christ was either Who He said He was, the Son of God, and equal with God, or He was the greatest liar that ever walked the face of the earth. Looking at the writings of Moses, and considering the confirmation of Moses by Jesus, we could apply the same statement to Moses, that is, that either he wrote the truth, or he was the biggest liar of all time, next to Jesus Himself.

"Few people, even the most outspoken critics of the Bible, are willing to go so far as to say that Jesus was the greatest liar of all time, in which case, they are admitting that He was indeed Who He said He was, in which case He could not lie. We must conclude therefore, that the writings of Moses are true and accurate. Our only problem then is to determine what he actually said, and what he left out because it was not pertinent to the purpose of his account."

CHAPTER III

Interpretation of Scripture

here is a growing gulf and even enmity between the Scientific community and Christianity. Not that this is anything new, but rather, is increasing in depth and intensity. The problem is primarily the result of the alignment of the Evolutionists and Scientists. Since evolution is basically in complete opposition to creation, the Christian community has rejected science almost in toto in order to avoid even the smallest concession to the theory of evolution.

"Much of the problem finds its roots in the dogmatic position taken by theologians on the one hand, and the more or less complete rejection of God as the Creator on the other hand. Many of the theories proposed by the scientific community are untenable. Likewise, in the religious or Christian community, there are alternatives to the traditional interpretations of Scripture which are just as Scriptural, but which are also confirmed by scientific observation. In other words, there are many areas in which Science and the Scriptures are in agreement, when one is willing to consider alternative interpretations of the Bible, especially when they are confirmed by more than one portion of the Scriptures.   ◆

"Unfortunately, Bible scholars, Christian leaders, and others are completely opposed to considering alternative interpretations on the grounds that it is an attempt to deny the Bible as the inspired word of God; or is a concession to the Evolutionists. Yet, we have many instances where it has been found that the meaning of the original texts is not properly presented in the older translations such as the King James version, and even in newer translations. Part of the problem lies in the fact that words do not always convey the true intended meaning. Furthermore, words may convey an idea which is understood by people of one culture, but may convey an entirely different meaning to people of another culture. Tradition, ethnic background, social conditions, all have a bearing on such interpretations.

"In other cases, words and statements are made, even in the Scriptures, which do not actually convey the truth. This may shock you, but consider this. We say that the sun rises in the East and sets in the West. Most people would say that this is true. Actually it is not. The earth turns on its axis so that the sun comes into view in the East and disappears from view in the West. Despite the fact that most people are aware of the truth of this, we accept the common expression because even though not factual, it is understood. The Bible uses this expression, of the sun rising and setting, in many places, even though it is not factual. Does that mean that the Bible is unreliable? Not at all. The people of that day, as today, understood the meaning intended. They would not have understood a reference to the earth rotating on its axis. The sun appears to rise and set, and speaking of it that way conveys all that is necessary.

"That this is true in other areas is quite apparent, as is the fact that words change their meaning according to the culture and state of civilization. So, with this in mind, I would like to present some suggestions of alternatives to the traditional interpretations of Scripture, where the meaning is not always clear or in sufficient detail.

"We are still talking about the introductory words in the Bible, 'In the beginning, God created the heavens and the earth.' Many diverse theories have been presented by science for the origin of the universe, but of these only two are at present competing seriously for acceptance. These are the STEADY-STATE theory and the BIG-BANG theory. The STEADY-STATE theory assumes that the universe is continually creating energy and/or matter out of the atoms, molecules and stray energy throughout the universe. Scientists further theorize that this process offsets the loss of energy and matter from decay. Even they cannot deny the observable fact that the universe is running down. Yet, the creation of new energy and/or matter remains only a theory. Additionally, this theory contradicts the laws of thermo-dynamics. There are many publications relative to this sub-ject, and in particular, Science Framework for California Schools,[1] (Sacramento).

"Astronomers in recent years have photographed many of the galaxies and interstellar areas using high powered telescopes such as the 100 inch Mt. Wilson and the 200 inch Mt. Palomer. These photographs have disclosed the fact that there are billions of galaxies in the universe, many of which are much larger than the one of which our solar system is a part. Spectrographic analyses have also been made of the light reaching earth from a number of these galaxies and suns in an effort to determine the chemical composition of these bodies. Two highly significant discoveries have resulted from this work. The first, was the dis-covery that the chemical composition of the distant galaxies was approximately the same as that of our own sun. That is, the distribution of the elements from the lightest to the heaviest is in about the same proportions regardless of the distance or age of these bodies. This is significant since many scientists have claimed that the heavier elements 'evolved' as it were, over the billions of years of the existence of the universe, being brewed in the atomic reactor of the sun's interior. It now appears that the elements of which the universe is composed have always been present in about the same relative proportions as they are today. Keep in mind that the light by which we now observe the distant galaxies has been traveling for a long time, and therefore, we are in effect looking back into time, since we see them as they were when the light left them, not as they are today."

At this point, Harry spoke up. "But don't most theologians reject this idea of great age for the universe? If the universe is really only a few thousand years old, how can we say that we are seeing distant galaxies as they were millions of years ago?" "That's a very good question," replied the Reverend, "but if you don't mind, let's hold that in abeyance until we finish looking at the creation theories. As I mentioned a moment ago, there were two discoveries resulting from the spectrographic analysis of the light reaching earth from distant galaxies. The second was the discovery that there was a shift in the wavelength of the light. This shift was toward the red end of the spectrum. An analogy would be the change in tone of a train whistle as the train reaches and then passes the listener. Only one conclusion can be drawn from this 'red shift' as it is called. The stars or galaxies showing this effect must be moving away from the earth, (or vice versa), at tremendous speeds. Calculations of the speed and distance of such galaxies from earth show that the universe is expanding in all directions from a central point in space. This leads to the conclusion that at one time, everything in the universe originated at that certain point in space. This has been estimated to have taken place perhaps 17 billion years ago.

"The name 'BIG BANG' comes from the conclusion that at that time, there was a tremendous explosion or 'Big Bang,' which threw the mass which now makes up our universe in every direction from the point of the explosion, and at tremendous speed. As this matter dispersed, there was a tendency for parts to be drawn together by mutual attraction through the force of gravity, thus forming galaxies of stars and planets which we can see today, and of which our earth is a part in the form of a satellite of our own star, the sun. Today, these stars and galaxies are still traveling away from the starting point, moving at various speeds and in every direction."

Now it was Jim who interrupted the Reverend. "But if that is the way things started, why haven't these galaxies all slowed down as time passed?" "Because there is no resistance to their travel," Reverend Spangler replied. "We have had this truth

14

brought home to us in the recent lunar flights and in the launching of the numerous man-made satellites, many of which are still circling the earth. As you are well aware, once these satellites are in orbit, they continue to travel at the same speed until slowed down by contact with air molecules high above the earth. The higher the orbit, the fewer the air molecules, and the longer it takes for the satellite to lose speed. On the lunar flight, the space craft continued at a speed which was affected only by the gravitational pull of the earth and/or moon. The galaxies on the other hand, are so far apart that the effects of gravitational pull is practically zero, between galaxies. Within the galaxies, the stars and planets travel in fixed orbits as they do in our own Milky Way.

"Besides the estimate of some 17 billion years for all of this to have taken place, measurements of the age of the earth, and more recently the moon, indicate an age of about 4½ billion years. Creationists immediately take issue with this, claiming that the Creator gave the earth, and the rest of the universe, the appearance of great age, 'to confound the wise.' They further refute the claims of astronomers that the light from distant galaxies has been traveling for millions or billions of years as the case requires. Instead, they claim that the Creator started light traveling from a point about 12,000 light years away, so that what we are seeing is the light which began to travel at that time. Since we are looking at the issue of the original creation, both as to source and time, let's look at some of the relative Scripture passages as contrasted with theories.

▪ "As I already mentioned, there are two major theories proposed by Science or perhaps I should say, atheistic scientists, to explain the origin of the universe. The steady-state theory fails at the outset since it contradicts the laws of thermodynamics. Furthermore, there is no evidence of any kind to support the theory, either from science or scripture. Now the question may be asked, 'is there any Scriptural basis for the BIG-BANG theory?'

"In Genesis 1:1 we read that, 'In the beginning, God created the heavens and the earth.' That is, God brought them into existence from nothing. All Creationists agree with this. In Psalm

15

33 Verse 6 we read, 'the worlds were framed by the *word* of God.' That is to say, God spoke and creation took place. The same passage continues with the statement, 'by the breath of His mouth all their host.' Now breath speaks of something in motion. Putting this together then, we have first of all the material of which our universe is composed being created by the spoken word, and secondly being put into motion by His breath. Isn't this exactly what we find described in the BIG-BANG theory? It was that moment in time when God spoke, bringing the universe into existence, and then putting everything in motion—a motion which we can see and measure right now. What a grand and magnificent picture of creation. And whether it took place 17 billion years ago or not makes no difference. The Scripture sets no time for this event, but since God is eternal, why must man try to limit Him to a few thousand years? •

"I should mention that the BIG-BANG theory as proposed by most Scientists completely ignores the Biblical account, creation and even God. However, this in no way means that there is no basis for the theory, as I just mentioned. The same astronomers who calculate an impending eclipse within seconds, and chart the passage of the shadow of the moon across the face of the earth in advance, are the same ones who found the 'red shift' and calculated the speed at which the galaxies are moving as well as the direction. We are perfectly willing to acclaim their abilities and accept the accuracy of their calculations on the one hand, but then discard completely their computations and observations on the other hand.

"In opposition to the scientific estimate of the age of the universe, there are several schools of thought among Creationalists and Theologians. As I already mentioned, one group takes the position that the universe is about 10,000 to 12,000 years old, and that the apparent age was purposely created to confuse the wise. Another group accepts the concept of great age for the universe, but interposes an indeterminate, but admittedly long period of time between the initial creation as set forth in Genesis 1:1 and the creative acts of Genesis 1:2-27. This is termed the 'gap' theory."

At this point Harry Bolin again spoke up. "I don't see where they find anything that even suggests such an intermediate period. I'll admit I am not as well grounded in the Bible as I ought to be, but I still don't see where they get that idea." "Actually," Reverend Spangler replied, "the idea of an intermediate period or 'gap' came about as a result of the discoveries in the field of paleontology, that is fossil remains of creatures which inhabited the earth at one time, apparently millions of years ago. In order to reconcile this observed evidence with the 'days' of creation in Genesis, some religious leaders concluded that there had been a tremendous cataclysm destroying everything on the face of the earth. Then at about 10,000 years ago, God created the things recorded in the book of Genesis."

"But that would mean there had been two creations, one millions of years ago, and another about 10,000 years ago," said Harry. "That's true," Reverend Spangler said, "and there is no basis in Scripture for believing in two separate creative periods. However, there are some Scriptures that are used to support this theory. Also, a great deal is made of the word which is translated into English as 'was' in Genesis 1:2. 'And the earth was without form and void.' Some have claimed that this should be translated as 'became,' thus suggesting that it had not always been in the described condition. It is further argued that the language suggests desolation and waste such as would result from a destructive cataclysm. While there is a great deal of geologic evidence which suggests one or more great cataclysmic events, it is also true that there are alternative interpretations which may be applied to this particular word. For instance, the same word could be rendered 'came into being.' That is to say in its primeval, created, uninhabitable state, the earth was without form and void. To put it still another way, the word referred to the earth as having no distinguishing feature or life of any kind. This is not only in complete agreement with Scriptural account, but also confirms the position taken by most Scientists in depicting the primeval earth as a shapeless mass devoid of life. The Berkeley translation of Genesis 2:5 puts it this way. 'When the Lord God made earth and heaven, there was not a shrub . . . nor any plant.' "

17

Harry again spoke up. "Do you mean to say that the 'gap' theory is based entirely on the use of the word 'was' in that portion of Scripture?" "No, there are two other passages commonly used to support this position," answered Reverend Spangler. "The first is found in the book of Jeremiah Chapter 4, verses 23–26, where we read, 'I beheld the earth, and, lo, it was without form and void.' The other passage is in Isaiah Chapter 24 and verse 1, where we read, 'The Lord maketh the earth empty, and maketh it waste, and turneth it upside down, and scattereth abroad the inhabitants thereof.' "

"Well, that does sound like the exact same language as Genesis uses," said Jim. "Yes," said the Reverend, "but one of the basic rules of Bible study is to look at everything in the light of its context. When we do this with the passage in Jeremiah, we find that this was specifically a message to the nation Israel. For instance, we read, 'declare ye in Judah . . . I will bring evil from the North . . . the destroyer of the Gentiles is on his way. . .' That's in Jeremiah 4:5-7. We also read, 'Lo, there was no man, and all the birds of the heavens were fled, and all the cities thereof were broken down.' That's in Jeremiah 4:25-26. Now even if we were to accept the premise that there had been a prior creation of animal life, (which is nowhere suggested or inferred), man is declared to have been created on the sixth day after the destruction of the original creation according to this theory. Add to this the reference to cities being broken down, and we can see that this passage in no way refers to a time prior to the creative acts recorded in Genesis.

"The book of Isaiah introduces another statement in connection with this assumed destruction of the earth. We read in Isaiah 4:2 and 3, '. . . as with the people, so with the priests . . . the land shall be utterly emptied . . .' We are forced to ask how this destruction could have included priests, when man himself had not been created as yet. And, even if man or a man-like creature had been previously created, the priesthood very definitely had not been established. Obviously then, this could not have reference to a time prior to the creation of man. I might also mention that there is mention of a desolation coming upon the earth in the book of II Kings, where this is definitely spoken of as future.

"The destruction and devastation depicted in the books of Jeremiah and Isaiah was in connection with the judgement to be brought upon the nation Israel as a result of its Spiritual condition, which could only be described as without form and void. This prophecy was literally fulfilled in the destruction of Jerusalem at a later date."

"That certainly puts a different light on the matter," said Jim, "but what I want to know is why God would have destroyed the earth, if indeed He did." "That's a very good question," answered Reverend Spangler, "and one that those who hold to this theory believe they have a good answer for. An important and integral part of this theory is the suggestion that the original creation was complete in every respect and suitable for habitation. However, when Satan rebelled against God, he took up his abode on the earth along with his fallen angels. As a result, the earth was thoroughly corrupted, making destruction the only means of cleansing it in order to make it suitable for man. However, the very same Scripture used to substantiate this theory, speaks of 'laws,' 'ordinances,' and 'everlasting covenant.' " Even the most naive student would not believe that these had been established during the presumed occupation of the earth by Satan and his angels.

"The fact of the matter is that the prophet Isaiah actually refutes the 'gap' theory. We read that, '(God) . . . created the heavens . . . formed the earth . . . established it . . . created it not in vain . . . formed it to be inhabited.' That's found in Isaiah 45:18. This clearly speaks of the original and only creation, since heavens and earth are both mentioned as being created. Of perhaps even greater importance is the use of the term 'established.' There can be only one meaning to this, and that is the idea of permanence or remaining. Add to this the statements that 'it was not in vain,' and was for the purpose of being inhabited, and we have irrefutable proof that there was no destruction of the earth prior to the creation account. Instead we find that the Bible itself emphasizes the fact that God created the earth for a purpose, and that purpose was for habitation by

19

man. God did not create it 'tohu,' that is, not a worthless thing or without a purpose. To suggest that God had created the earth complete and ready for habitation by man, and then destroyed it, also suggests that the original creation had been a complete failure, thus discrediting both God and the Bible. Theologically, we acknowledge that God makes no mistakes. Yet, we find that the Creationists and Theologians who claim that the earth *became* without form and void as a result of judgement upon Satan, also believe and accept the fact that Satan is still very active in the world today. This then leads to the only possible conclusion, that if God did indeed destroy His original creation, it was all to no avail. Satan is still here, and the whole creation process had to be repeated over again.

"A very strong argument against the 'gap' theory is the use of the copulative 'and' at the beginning of the second verse. Of course, you realize that in the original manuscripts, there was no division into separate verse. In other words, the second verse of Genesis 1 continues the account of verse 1. This becomes of even greater significance in connection with the question of the word translated 'day' in the Genesis account. We will look into that in greater detail later.

"A final argument against the 'gap' theory is the fact that Scripture clearly speaks of but one creation, frequently preceding the word with the article 'the.' Thus, there could not have been an earlier creation which was destroyed, since there would then be two separate creations, one before the assumed destruction and one following."

The Reverend paused as if reflecting on the things he had just said, and Jim took this opportunity to speak up. "You know," he said, "I was thinking as you were talking that we have no real conception of God. Oh, I know, we have a revelation of Him through Jesus Christ, but I mean what He must look like, or where He is, or especially how big He is to have created this entire universe, which in itself is bigger than our minds can comprehend."

The Reverend thought for a moment and then said, "That of course, has been one of the great questions facing man from the very beginning. I'd like to suggest a possible answer, but it is getting late. Why don't we adjourn for tonight and continue this next week at the same time." "That sounds great to me," said Harry. "Me too," said Jim, "but the only trouble is that I can hardly wait for the next session. These are things that I have wondered about ever since I became a Christian. Thanks Pastor, for taking the time to talk to us about these things. See you next week." And with this parting remark, Harry and Jim reluctantly left for home.

CHAPTER IV

Creation vs. Evolution

 week after the events of the preceding chapter, Jim Martin and Harry Bolin were once again seated in Reverend Spangler's sitting room. The Reverend began the discussions by referring to the subject they had been discussing at the close of the previous meeting. "We were talking about the person and personality of God last week. The only source of real information on this subject of course, is the Bible, and the one clear statement concerning Him which is pertinent to our thinking is the statement that, 'God is a Spirit.' Now this makes it very clear that God is not human in any sense of the word, and in fact is not a being having a physical body of any kind.

"In order to even begin to comprehend this, we must first of all consider this universe in which we live, and note what it is made of. We all know that everything is composed of molecules, which in turn are composed of atoms, which in turn are made up of electrons, protons, and neutrons. Secondly, we find that all of these are held together by forces which we do not fully understand but which we shall call electromagnetic forces. We also know, as Einstein showed, that matter and energy are essentially the same thing. Einstein's formula to demonstrate this was $E = MC^2$. In simple terms this means that matter may be converted into energy yielding an amount which is the product of multiplying the mass by speed of light squared. In other words, our entire universe is really energy, either in a static form which we call matter, or as energy itself such as light, heat, and motion plus gravitation and the intermolecular energy which hold the electrons and atoms in orbit. We might simply call our universe an electromagnetic dimension.''

"Just what do you mean by dimension?" asked Jim. "Well, we all know," said the Reverend, "that we look at the solid material in our universe as having height, width, and depth. That is three dimensions. However, scientists have suggested that we should add a fourth, time. Others have suggested that there may be more than one co-existent universe having such different properties that one is not aware of the other, nor is there any conflict or interaction between them. I know this is hard to understand, and probably our finite minds are just not capable of doing so. Nevertheless, if we assume that such different dimensions or diverse universes do exist, we can perhaps in a small way understand God and His heaven. I think it is rather significant that in 1 Corinthians 2:9 a statement is made which seems to fit this thought exactly. We read, 'eye hath not seen, nor ear heard, neither have entered into the heart of man, the things which God hath prepared for them that love Him.' Obviously this is speaking of Heaven and Spiritual things to come. Certainly we human beings cannot imagine what such a diverse universe is like, even though in the book of the Revelation some inkling is given of what to expect. But how can we picture a universe not based on the electromagnetic principle with its electrons, atoms, and molecules plus all the electromagnetic forms of energy with which we are familiar? Very likely this other universe is so much larger than ours that it might be likened to a comparison between a molecule and a solar system. I don't know. But I am convinced that God's Heaven is co-existent with our universe. There are many portions of Scripture which suggest this, such as in Ephesians 4:6-10. You might want to read that passage when you have time."

"That's certainly an approach I had never considered," said Harry, "although I have heard the suggestion that there might be more than one co-existent universe with ours. As you say, that would explain why the Bible says 'no man hath seen God at any time.' This would also explain some of the other strange things in Scripture such as Moses' experience on Mt. Sinai, and Elisha's ability to see horses and chariots surrounding the place where he was, things which his servant could not see until Elisha prayed that God would open the servant's eyes. These are wonderful, but sobering thoughts, Reverend." "Thank you," Reverend Spangler said. "But I want you to understand that this is just a theory on my part. I cannot prove that this is actually the case, even though it does seem to be confirmed, at least in part, by Scripture. However, let's get back to the Creation account.

"I think you will agree that from all the evidence, both scientific and Scriptural, we must conclude that our universe came into existence by a creative act of God perhaps seventeen billion years ago, and that the galaxies with all their stars and planets have been moving in various directions and orbits ever since. The known universe is continuing to expand, and there is no reason to believe that it will some day stop expanding and shrink back to a central point in space. The question of age of the universe is linked directly to the Genesis account in which the word 'day' is used as the period during which certain events took place.

"In the book of Exodus, Chapter 20, Verse 11, we read a simple yet, majestic statement which sets the stage for one of the most controversial subjects in the whole of Scripture. We read, 'in six days God made heaven and earth, the sea, and all that in them is . . .' The controversy is not with regard to the creation itself, but rather to the meaning and interpretation of the word translated 'day.' However, before looking at this aspect of the matter, there are two questions which should be examined and if possible answered. First of all, is the question of whether any one interpretation or view regarding the 'days' of the creation account is essential to salvation. There are those who feel

25

that a person must hold to their particular interpretation in order to be saved.

"Now salvation, as taught in the Scriptures, is the process or act by which any person accepts the free gift, by faith, of redemption, whereby he is forgiven of his sins and made a child of God with all the privileges and future blessings which such a relationship provides. This free gift is, of course, provided by the death and resurrection of Jesus Christ, Who came to earth and took upon Himself the form of man, and then gave His life as ransom for many. Acceptance of this substitutionary death and resurrection constitutes salvation.

"There is nothing in any of the Scriptures which places a particular interpretation of Scripture as a conditional requirement for salvation as far as the subject of the days of creation is concerned. Therefore, we may conclude that regardless of one's interpretation of the Genesis account, anyone can be saved by the simple act of faith in Jesus Christ as Savior and Lord.

"The second question has to do with God's ability. There are two main interpretations of the Genesis account of creation. One holds that the 'days' of Genesis 1 and 2 were literal solar days of 24 hours, more or less, each. The other is that these 'days' were ages or periods of time. So, the question is, 'could God have created the universe and everything in it in six, 24-hour days?' We are forced to answer in the affirmative if we accept the Bible as the inspired word of God, since we read that 'with God all things are possible.' On the other hand, could God have created the universe and then brought about the things recorded in Genesis 1 over a very long period of time? In other words, 'is God limited in time?' Again we would have to answer, 'with God all things are possible.' Now, since there are two *possible* interpretations as far as God's ability is concerned regarding the length of time during which creation was accomplished, we need to look further to determine as far as possible, which of the two interpretations appears to conform more nearly to other parts of Scripture, and if possible, is supported by other evidence.

"To the vast majority of people today, the controversy between the scientific world and religion, as it is held forth by those who believe that the Bible is the inspired word of God, has already been settled. Newspapers, periodicals, scientific articles and textbooks used in various institutions of learning, not only speak of evolution as an accepted, proven fact, but also refer to the Bibical account as a myth.[2]

"A national magazine in a report on scientific expeditions repeatedly refers to evolutionary processes as proven facts, when actually they are the deductions made as a result of certain limited observations of present day conditions. The same society carries this to an even greater degree in its televised programs.

"I mention this, because Science completely rejects the concept of six, 24-hour days of creation, as dogmatically held by many religious leaders. This then has led to a complete rejection of the entire creation account as having been a direct series of acts by a Supreme Being. The alternative then has been the theories proposed by Science in an effort to explain the origin of the universe and more specifically of life.

"Now let's look at some of the arguments used by those Creationists who claim that the 'days' of Genesis 1 were periods of 24 hours or a solar day. Pember[3], who is perhaps typical of this group, states that the Bible does not say that the initial creation of Genesis 1:1 was part of the first day. He further states that the six days described in Genesis 1, beginning at verse 2, were six 24-hour days. Yet, in the book of Exodus we read, 'for in six days the Lord made Heaven and earth, the sea and all that in them is.'[4] Now in Genesis 1:5, the first day ended after the light was divided from the darkness. Either this first day included the initial creative act, or it took more than six days for *all* of creation, as stated in Genesis 2:2 and 3. Therefore, if the initial creative act was indeed part of the first day, and if according to the 'gap' theory there was an undetermined period of time between the initial creation and the special created acts recorded in Genesis, then this first day must of necessity have been one of extremely long duration. This then, places these theorists in a real dilemma, since they claim that the 'day' of Genesis was a 24-hour day. It would make no sense to claim that the first 'day' was a very long period, while the others were normal 24-hour days.

"I think you can see from this, that according to Scripture, the initial creation was part of the first day. There is no suggestion of a gap between this event and the creative or forming acts which followed. This leads back to our original question as to whether these were six 24-hour periods or six periods of undetermined length."

At this point in the discussions, Mrs. Spangler came in with a tray holding a pot of tea and some cookies, which brought the talks to a halt. The hour was getting late by the time these had been consumed, so Jim and Harry took their leave, thanking the Reverend and his wife for the fellowship and refreshments. "See you again next week at the same time," the Reverend said as they left the house. "I'd like to continue coming with Jim, if it's alright with you," said Harry. "Of course," the Reverend said, "and don't hesitate to ask any questions that come to mind in the meantime." "Don't worry," Harry said, "I'm not bashful about doing that. Good night and thanks again."

CHAPTER V

Earth's Age

A nother week had passed, and Reverend Spangler was seated with his friends, Harry Bolin and Jim Martin in the minister's living room.

"Last week," Reverend Spangler began, "we were considering the arguments concerning the length of the days mentioned in the first Chapter of Genesis. Actually, there are three principle uses in Scripture of the word translated 'day.' The first is, of course, the common use meaning a period of 24 hours. The second is considered by some to be the period during which God revealed the Genesis account to Moses. The third is that of an indefinite period of time including an eon or age. In practice, the word 'day' is used in many ways in Scripture. For example:

1. 'Light' is called 'day.'
2. Evening and morning.
3. Day of the Lord.
4. Day as a thousand years.
5. Day of His wrath.

6. Day of visitation.

A very strong argument to show that a 24-hour day was not the intended meaning of the 'days' of Genesis 1 is found in Genesis 2 verses 4 and 5 where we read, '. . . in the *day* that the Lord God made the earth and the Heavens, and every plant . . .' Now, if the word translated 'day' means a 24-hour period, we have here a contradiction in Scripture of the highest order. Certainly it could not be concluded that the entire creation took place within 24 hours or one day as these two verses state. Thus, we have here irrefutable proof that the word translated 'day' can and does have a much broader meaning than the limited meaning usually ascribed to it.

"In view of what I have just mentioned, how can we be dogmatic about this matter of the length of the days of creation? Shouldn't we then give consideration to the alternatives, as long as they do not contradict Scripture? If one is willing to accept this broader interpretation of the word 'day,' as meaning an extended period of time, there is an amazing correlation between the Biblical account and the findings of Science. We are speaking now simply of the time involved, not the relative merits of the theory of evolution versus creation.

"I should mention that there are some who will offer an exception to the foregoing as a result of the use of the preposition 'in' used in Exodus 20:11, where this word is italicized, indicating that it was inserted by the translators to clarify the passage. Leaving it out causes the passage to read, 'For six days the Lord made Heaven and earth, the sea and all that in them is . . .' When this is coupled with the use of the word 'made' instead of 'created,' they claim that this refers to the work process which God carried out following the initial creation and subsequent destruction as suggested by the 'gap' theory. Yet, nowhere else in Scripture are the Heavens and earth said to have been made. They were created according to Genesis 1:1. Therefore, the passage in question refers to the entire creative program which included the initial creation of the Heavens and earth, and the subsequent forming, making or creating of everything else.

"I think we would do well to consider for a moment the difference between the words translated 'made,' 'formed,' and 'created.' Some have made a great deal of the different uses of these words as they apply to the creation account. In Genesis 2:4 we read, that '. . . the Heavens and . . . the earth . . . were created . . . the Lord God made the earth and the Heavens.' Now as you know, a thing cannot be made or formed unless there is something from which to make it, which in turn would require creation. In Genesis 1:21, whales are said to have been 'created,' but later, in the 25th verse, animals are said to have been 'made.' While there is certainly some latitude in translating, the mere fact that both words are used of the same creative act indicates that the writer intended to convey the thought that whereas the initial act was one of creation, in the sense of being made from nothing, the following acts were creation in the sense that they had never existed previously in that form. They were entirely new, yet, made from already existing material. Man himself is said to have been 'made' from the dust of the earth (Genesis 2:7), but he is also said to have been created (Genesis 1:27).

"Another fact of considerable importance which bears on the case is that the first verse of the Bible does not appear to be a compendium or summary of what follows. Rather, it is a simple statement to the effect that the first act of creation was that of bringing the universe into existence out of nothing. This included everything necessary for the 'creation,' 'making,' or 'forming' of everything else that followed. The time required, the date of this act, and the possible preparatory stages through which it may have gone are not mentioned or even suggested. If, as the scientific community holds, this took billions of years, is that too long for an eternal God?

"Despite the complete lack of Scriptural proof, there are those who adhere doggedly to the belief that creation took place some 10,000 to 12,000 years ago. They attempt to explain away all scientific evidence to the contrary by means of discrepancies between the findings of various investigators. They take the position that since Scientists are not in complete agreement with regard to the age of fossils, the geologic column, rocks, etc., none of the findings are acceptable. Yet, on the other hand, when the same methods which are claimed to be unreliable are used and confirm a certain theological position, they are gladly accepted and hailed as proof of the interpretation claimed by these theologians. For instance, the Carbon 14 method of dating has been used to date many artifacts and archeological finds. When the results confirm the claim of the theologians they are received with joy, but when the same method suggests, for example, that the earth is far older than 12,000 years, the method is claimed to be unreliable.

"What I am saying is that we ought to be consistent in our thinking. It is true that the Carbon 14 method of dating is not always reliable. In recent years specimens of wood obtained from Mt. Ararat above the 14,000 foot level were examined to determine if they could have been part of Noah's Ark. Carbon 14 tests gave an apparent age of about 3,000 years. However, additional tests by other methods gave an age of about 5,000 years which would agree with the accepted time of the flood."

"Are you saying that the Carbon 14 method is of no value in measuring the age of artifacts?" asked Harry. "No. I am simply saying that this method should be supplemented by other methods," the Reverend answered. "What other methods of dating are being used?" Jim asked. "There are any number of methods, including tree ring dating, radioactivity and chemical analysis. The method used depends on the estimated age, such as exposure of the specimen to weathering, chemical change, chemical action. In recent years, radioactive dating has been developed to a remarkable degree. Harry, you are probably familiar with some of those methods since they fall under the classification of chemistry."

"Well," Harry said, "that's a little out of my field, but I have read something on the subject, and I know that it is based primarily on the known fact that radioactive materials decay, or gradually lose their radioactivity over specific periods of time. For instance, a certain substance may lose half of its radioactivity in let's say 100 years. Half of the remainder will be lost in the next 100 years. In this process, part of the substance is changed to a more stable element. By determining the ratio of changed to unchanged material, the age can be estimated with a fair degree of accuracy."

Now Jim added his voice to the discussion. "If this method is reliable, why don't the Creationists accept it?" "Well," Harry said "like the Carbon 14 method, everyone does not always come up with the exact same answer, and so if the results tend to contradict the claims of the Creationists they reject it completely. Granted that there may be some discrepancies in this method, and also granted that there may also be some difference in the assumed rate of radioactive decay. Still, these discrepancies could not even begin to account for the tremendous difference between the age of rocks and fossils determined by this method, and the assumed age of the earth of 10,000 to 12,000 years.

"Reverend Spangler, you stated earlier in our talks that the age of the earth as well as the moon had been estimated to be about four and a half billion years. If, as many Creationists claim, the earth is only 10,000 years old, then the error in the methods used to arrive at 4½ billion years would have to be of the order of one million to one. To put it another way, if the Creationists are right, then the radioactive dating method must be in error by as much as a million times the actual age. I'll grant that there is possibly some latitude for error in making determinations of such a sophisticated nature, but a million times error from the truth? I have more respect than that for man's intelligence."

"Thanks for those comments, Harry," Reverend Spangler said. "And in addition to the actual determinations of the age of the earth by the radioactive method, we all know that the surface of the earth itself gives the appearance of great age. As we observe the effects of erosion, weathering, sedimentation, uplift, crustal movement, continental drift, subsidence, and volcanic activity, we see every indication that the present features of the earth's surface are the result of a very long period of exposure to the forces of nature. Since the beginning of recorded history, the changes that have taken place are very slight, yet we can see that very great changes have taken place, and must have required extremely long periods of time.

"A very good example of this is found in the tremendous sedimentary deposits found in many parts of the world. Some of these are many thousands of feet in depth."

"But isn't it these very sediments that the Creationists claim prove the worldwide extent of the flood?" Jim asked. "Yes," answered the Reverend, "but their arguments will not hold water. (No pun intended.) Even an amateur, looking at an exposed sedimentary deposit, such as a cut in a bank, can see at once that the sediments are not of uniform sized particles. There are layers of fine sand, silt, fine gravel, coarse gravel and perhaps even larger rocks. The layers may be very thin strata or very thick, and usually of varying thickness. Anyone who has studied or even observed how strata of sand or gravel is deposited knows that the faster a moving body of water travels, the coarser the gravel that it may move or carry. Fine silt is deposited by water that is practically at rest such as the bottom of a lake or the ocean. In a recent televised program about Noah's ark, an astronomer was questioned about possible causes for the flood. He replied that the approach or collision of a large meteor with the earth could have caused the oceans to be thrown completely from their basins, inundating the highest mountains. I submit that such a catastrophic event would *not* have left the stratified layers of sand, silt, gravel, and rocks found all over the world. Some years ago, in Mesopotamia, archeologists uncovered a layer of silt some eleven feet thick, with artifacts of an ancient civilization above *and* below the layer of silt, but with none in the layer of silt. They hailed this as positive proof of the flood. This is certainly very possible in view of the length of time during which the flood waters covered the earth as stated in Genesis."

At this point Jim interrupted the discussion with a question. "What about the sedimentary deposits found high in many of the mountains of the earth? Isn't this proof that they were deposited by the flood?" Reverend Spangler hesitated a moment, and then said, "No, I do not agree with that hypothesis. Consider this. Sediments are carried from higher elevations to lower elevations by moving water and/or wind. Even after a tidal wave, little if any silt or debris is left on the high points covered by the wave, because the rapidly moving water carries such material back when it recedes. In the case of sedimentary deposits found in high mountains, these are always stratified, contains strata of various size particles, and frequently also contains fossils."

"But isn't this positive proof that these mountains were covered with water by the flood?" asked Jim.

"It is certainly proof that at some time these mountains were under water, but not by a flood. As I mentioned before, a tidal wave, or any rapidly moving mass of water would carry everything along with it, and would not deposit silt or fine sand in uniform strata covering extensive areas. In any case, the speed of the moving water determines the size of the particles which the water can transport. For instance, in mountain areas where streams flow rapidly, fairly large stones can be transported. As the stream reaches lower elevations and begins to level out, it can only carry small stones and sand. When the stream becomes a lake or empties into the sea, the very smallest particles which settle as silt, eventually deposit. Thus, an examination of sediments can reveal the speed of the flowing water which produced them. Now if the sedimentary deposits found at high elevations were the result of the flood, they would be basically fine sediments, since the Biblical account indicates that the waters rose slowly over a period of months. There is nothing in the account to indicate that the water moved rapidly or was like a tidal wave. The very presence of fossils, which many hold to be proof of the flood, in fact refutes the claim that these sediments were deposited by the flood waters. Fossils are heavy as compared with silt, and could only have been carried by rapidly moving water or left as skeletons of animals in that environment."

"Couldn't this be taken as proof that the flood waters did cover the area long enough for these forms of life to have lived and died there?" Jim asked.

"No, I do not think so," said the Reverend. "In the first place, the flood waters covered the earth for a period of several months. Since the waters rose slowly according to the Genesis account, they would not have carried mature mollusk for example. Rather, only embryonic forms of shellfish could have floated and been carried to the high mountains. These could not possibly have developed and grown to the size or profusion actually found as fossils today. Secondly, if it were assumed that the rising flood waters were so turbulent that they carried all kinds and great quantities of sea creatures with it to deposit them at high elevations, they would be in a hodgepodge mixture in one great sedimentary layer. Instead, the fossils are found more or less as if catalogued, with the simpler forms in the lowest strata, and progressively higher or more complex forms in successive, higher levels. This is the basis for the geologic column, and while there may be some question as to the *exact* age of each strata or any particular life form represented by the fossils, there can be no doubt that they were deposited over a vast period of time, as shown by the nature and extent of the sediments. The most amazing part of this is that this graduation of life forms from the simpler to the more complex, supports the Biblical account as they were created eon after eon.''

Now Harry spoke up. "Doesn't Science base much of its dating methods on the Uniformitarian theory? In other words, that the changes observed in the earth's surface took place at a more or less uniform rate over the millions of years."

"That is more or less true," said the Reverend, "although Science recognizes that the rate of sedimentation, as well as other natural forces varies, depending on many factors such as volcanic activity, siesmic disturbances, weather, sun spots, or proximity of extraterrestrial bodies. But in most cases these are short period influences. Sedimentary deposits represent the accumulation of tremendous quantities of material resulting from the disintegration or weathering of solid rock masses. This weathering and disintegration takes place at a fairly consistent rate, and extremely slowly. The flood would have had very little effect on this process. Only sediments already in existence as a result of eons of weathering, glaciation, and volcanic activity would have been transported by the flood waters.

"Since the sedimentary rocks and deposits are the obvious result of eons of geologic activity, some Creationists go so far as to suggest that these were part of the creation which took place 10,000 to 12,000 years ago, and again were placed there to confuse the wise. Unfortunately for them, the same type of sediment formation is taking place before our very eyes, and we can measure the rate of such processes. I am convinced that Science has given us the true answer as to how and when these sedimentary rocks and deposits were formed, and I can see no conflict with the Biblical account, but rather complete confirmation. Over the millions of years since the initial creation, rocks have been disintegrating and weathering, forming vast quantities of gravel, sand, and rock dust. Much of this was carried by the rivers and streams into the lakes and seas where they accumulated and formed strata upon strata of various density, particle size, and thickness, depending on conditions at the time. Over milleniums of time, some of these sedimentary deposits were lifted by the titanic forces still at work in the earth's crust. This was the period of mountain building, thrusting earth masses thousands of feet above sea level. This process is still at work, and the rate of elevation or lowering of mountain ranges has been measured by very sophisticated instruments. What I am saying, is that there is every indication that the process of sedimentation is not something which took place as a result of the flood, and at no other time. Instead, it has been going on ever since the initial creation of the earth, and still continues, following the natural laws which the Creator established at that time. Another fact in this connection is that of the fossil fuels, gas, coal, and oil, which are found in connection with sedimentary deposits. Some Creationists claim these were laid down at the time of the flood. This would also mean that the sediments themselves were laid down at the same time, yet, as we have just noted, this is not the case. Besides the varied composition of the strata, thus, indicating various times and conditions during their deposition, we also find limestone strata frequently associated with the fossil fuels. These limestone formations could not possibly have been carried by the flood waters, or laid down during the few months they covered the earth. The Bible itself completely refutes this theory, since in Genesis 6:14 Noah is told to cover the inside and outside of the ark with pitch."

"But are we sure they used bitumen and not tree sap?" asked Jim.

"The most competent authorities tell us that this was bitumen, and according to the reports on the pieces of wood recovered from Mt. Ararat, claimed to be from the ark, it was indeed bitumen. Now as I'm sure you could tell us Harry," Reverend Spangler continued, "bitumen is one of the products derived

37

from natural oil deposits. In many places, crude oil seeps to the surface of the earth from deposits deep down below. This forms pools of oil which gradually form a thick, tarry surface. The LaBrea tar pits in Los Angeles is an excellent example of this. We also know now that there are tremendous oil reserves under the surface of the earth in the Arabian peninsula, where Noah built his ark. Since we have ample evidence from Scripture that pitch was available before the flood, it would be contradicting the Bible to claim that fossil fuels were laid down at the time of the flood. Thus, we see that sedimentary rocks are in no way indicative of the flood. The only sediments which appear to have any bearing on the flood are those uncovered in Mesopotamia as I mentioned earlier, and this consisted of one uniform layer of silt. We should mention too, that if, at this low elevation, the sedimentary deposit was eleven feet thick, we would certainly not expect to find sedimentary rocks thousands of feet thick on the high mountains. However, the hour is getting late, so I suggest we disband once more and meet next week at this same time." And with this, the small group left for their respective homes.

CHAPTER VI

Science and the Bible

nly Jim Martin appeared one week later at the Reverend Spangler's home. "Where's Harry?" asked the Reverend.

"He couldn't make it tonight," Jim answered. "But he expects to be here next week. He sends his regrets."

"Sorry he couldn't make it Jim, but we can go ahead anyway if you wish." "I'd like that very much, Pastor," said Jim, "and I'll brief Harry during the week on our discussion."

"Well," began the Reverend, "we were discussing the various arguments about the age of the earth last week, and I'd like to tell you about some additional evidence, that in my opinion, proves conclusively that the earth is indeed millions of years old, and certainly not merely 10,000 to 12,000 years old.

"A very good example is a place called Specimen Ridge in Yellowstone National Park. In an area of some forty square miles are fossil remains of forests that once covered that part of our country. In one place, partly exposed by cliffs, *twenty-seven* forests lie buried, one atop the other in about 2,000 feet of compressed volcanic ash and mud.[5] Any attempt to explain this as having been created in situ, or that it is the result of the flood, could only place such a person in the position of one who has already made up his mind and doesn't want to be influenced by facts. The presence of volcanic ash between the layers or strata indicates the origin and means by which the forests were buried. More important is the inescapable truth that forests do not spring up and grow overnight in a devastated area. For 27 forests in succession to have sprung up and matured, one atop the other, would have taken a very long time. Not to mention the time required for the forests to be buried, converted to stone, and then to become exposed to view through the elevation of the land mass, followed by the erosion necessary to do this."

Jim spoke up at this point to ask a question. "Isn't this the sort of thing that the proponents of the 'gap' theory use to prove their theory? It seems to me that this is a rather strong argument for their case, since they claim that God destroyed everything on the earth."

"Not really," the Reverend answered, "because this particular evidence would then suggest twenty-seven separate destructions. Proponents of the 'gap' theory hold that in the beginning, God created the Heavens and the earth, and made the earth completely suitable for habitation by man. Included in this creation were animals whose fossil remains we now find scattered over many parts of the earth. Then, Satan, being cast out of heaven, took up his abode on the earth in a place called Eden. However, Satan and the fallen angels who followed him, polluted the earth to such an extent that God found it necessary to destroy everything on the earth, making it a desolate waste. During one of our discussions I pointed out the fallacy of their arguments. In addition, I would like to call your attention to another Scripture which they use in support of their theory. This is found in Ezekiel 28:13, where we read, 'You lived in Eden, the garden of God.' A careful study of this passage shows that this was addressed to the King of Tyre, but was actually addressed to Satan. There are other instances of this type of address in the Bible, including the New Testament. However, the point I want to make, is that Eden was the place where God placed

Adam and Eve. Now, if God had destroyed the earth prior to the creative acts in Genesis 1:2-27, how could Eden have been a place that existed prior to that destruction? Did God destroy the earth, and then turn right around and rebuild the earth almost exactly as it had been before, including a place called Eden? This makes no sense at all, and in fact actually questions both the wisdom and power of God. On the other hand, the Scripture is clear that Satan was in the garden of Eden with Adam and Eve, and it was his activities there that brought about judgment.

"There is still one other argument used by the proponents of an age of 10,000 to 12,000 years for the earth. This is based on the expression found in the creation account, 'evening and morning.' This expression was used by the Israelites to signify the beginning and ending of a 24-hour period, from the evening of one day and ending with the evening of the next. However, this expression could also have indicated the beginning and ending of a period of time during which certain events took place. That this is the intended meaning in the creation account seems evident from the fact that the statement does not say 'was a day,' or 'was *one* day.' In fact, the King James translation says '*were* the . . . day.'

The New American Standard uses the expression, 'there was evening and there was morning, a . . . day.'

"Some claim that the use of both expressions, that is 'day' and 'evening and morning,' coupled together, is proof that it was indeed a 24-hour day. However, there is no other place in Scripture where a double emphasis is placed on 'day' to distinguish it as a 24-hour period. An even more positive proof is provided in Genesis 2:4 and 5 where we read, '. . . in the *day* that the Lord God made earth and Heaven.' Now, if the word translated 'day' means a 24-hour period, as I said earlier in our talks, we have here a contradiction of the highest order.

"The Bible is sometimes referred to as 'The Book of Words,' whereas the universe, including the earth, might be called 'The Book of Works.' Someone has said that while the Bible is not a book on Science, where it speaks on scientific matters it is completely reliable. We might consider the Bible as the outline, where it speaks on creation, whereas geology fills in many of the details. With this in mind, and using the broader interpretation of the word 'day' in the Genesis account, we find that there can be perfect harmony between the Biblical account and the scientific position with reference to the presence of fossils and the geologic column.''

''Just what is the geologic column?'' Jim asked. ''You mentioned it before, but I'd like to know just what the term means.''

''Well,'' answered the Reverend, ''as I pointed out in discussing sedimentary deposits and rocks, we find that fossils found in these are more or less 'catalogued,' that is, simpler life forms are represented in the lowest levels, which obviously are the oldest, followed by progressively more complex forms in successively higher, and thus, more recent levels. This is called the geologic column, and Scientists feel that it represents the development of more and more complex life forms from the earliest times to more recent times. Some Creationists claim that sometimes the order is reversed, and therefore, the geologic column is completely unreliable.

''While it is true that the order is occasionally found reversed, this is the result of crustal folding, in which the crust of the earth has been not only pushed upwards, but has actually been folded completely over, thus, turning the sedimentary rocks upside down. This effect can be seen in many areas as one travels around our country, especially in the western part of the U.S. Sometimes the strata are tilted, sometimes standing on end, and in other cases, as I just mentioned, folded completely over. Despite this, the overwhelming preponderance of sedimentary rocks do display the geologic column with the simpler life forms represented in the lowest levels and the progressively higher forms in successively higher levels.''

''Does the Biblical account in any way support this?'' asked Jim.

''Yes it does,'' said Reverend Spangler. ''The Biblical account gives the order of creation as, first, plant life, followed in succession by invertebrate, fish, amphibia, insects, reptiles of land, sea and air, mammals of land, sea and air, true birds, and finally man. That is, He created all life forms beginning with the simpler forms and ending with the most complex. Every applicable field of Science confirms this. But there is one more example of visible evidence to show that the earth is indeed far older than the suggested 10,000 years. However, if you don't mind, I'd like to postpone our discussion of that until next week.

"Do you think Harry will be coming with you next week?" asked Reverend Spangler. "Yes, I'm sure he will," said Jim, and with this he departed.

It was a week later when the three met again. The Reverend spoke. "In addition to the geologic column and the wide distribution of fossil evidence around the world, certain specific fossil remains have a pronounced bearing on the question of the age of the earth as well as the mode of deposition. Reference has already been made to the petrified forests of Yellowstone National Park. Of even greater significance are the deposits of Diatomaceous earth found in many localities. This unique material consists of the microscopic skeletons of diatoms, primarily certain algae, and radiolaria. These skeletons are so small that they may only be observed individually under a high-powered microscope. The Diatomaceous earth, formed by the depositing of billions upon billions of these skeletons, can be ground into a powder so fine that it is used in making various polishes. In spite of the microscopic size of the individual skeletons, there are deposits hundreds of feet thick, such as those at Lompoc, California. There is but one way in which such extensive deposits could have been formed, and that is by the existence of successive generations of the plants and animals whose skeletons make up the deposits over very long periods of time. The indestructible skeletons of these life forms gradually settled to the bottom of the waters in which they lived and died, forming what is termed "diatomaceous ooze" or "radiolarian ooze." These deposits are formed only on the bottom of water. They are still being formed today in many places, often at depths greater than 10,000 feet, and at a rate of about one-half inch per thousand years.

"Now, for the benefit of opponents of uniformatarianism, let me hasten to add that it is indeed possible that the rate at which these deposits were formed was at one time greater than today. However, even if we were to consider that the rate at which these enormous deposits were formed was ten times the present rate, (and there is not the slightest evidence that this was so), it would still have taken 120,000 years to deposit 100 feet of material, loosely compacted. Under the conditions at which these deposits are formed, the skeletons of the Radiolaria are deposited in almost pure form since the calcarous shells of the Foraminifera which accompany the Radiolaria are dissolved at these greater depths.[6] Regardless of the depth at which the original deposits of Diatomaceous material was formed, we are forced to accept the fact that these deposits were at some time raised above the level of the sea and subsequently exposed, or at least made accessible to mining operations somewhere above sea level. Therefore, we must take into account both the time required for the countless generations of microscopic plants and animals to go through their life cycles, die, and be deposited in enormous quantities, and the geologic processes whereby these deposits were compressed into more or less rock-like layers, and finally the time during which these deposits were elevated above sea level.

"To suggest that the deposits of Diatomaceous earth were formed during the time the flood covered the earth is preposterous, with no possible support from either science or the Bible. While it might have been possible for a colony of these microscopic creatures to have lived and reproduced even several generations over the period of the flood, by no stretch of the imagination could these extensive deposits have been left behind in so short a time.

"There may be those who would suggest that the flood waters, which might include tidal waves, carried skeletal remains of the creatures from a wide area and then dumped them in the confined locations where we now find them. Such a suggestion is not only without foundation, but is impossible because of the very nature of these fossils. Mixed with water, these microscopic particles remain suspended in water for a considerable length of time, particularly when there is any agitation of the water such as would be the case with a flood or tidal wave. More likely, the particles would have been carried out to sea by the receding waters even if they had been concentrated in one area.

Furthermore, the deposits are found with the individual skeletons cemented together as a result of secretions, chemical solution and deposition. This could not happen except by prolonged contact under pressure, thus, attributing to the fact that they were formed at some ocean depth over very long periods of time. Disregarding the flood theory of the formation and distribution of fossils, we must likewise conclude that it would also have been impossible for such immense deposits to have been formed within the 12,000-year period suggested by some Creationists. This is even more apparent when we take into account the time required for elevation of the land masses where these deposits are found.

"Someone has suggested[7] that the earth, immediately after the appearance of the dry land in Genesis 1:9, consisted of a single continent surrounded by water. It is further contended by the same lecturer that this condition continued up to the time of the flood. I previously pointed out that according to the Genesis account there were mountains and high mountains already before the flood. The basis for the position taken by this same individual is that the only way in which the created animals could multiply over the face of the earth would be if there was but one continent. There is in fact considerable scientific and geologic evidence that the land surface of the earth was at one time a single great continent, but that through continental drift, subsidence and uplift, this broke up into the continents as we know them today. Recent research and study of the floor of the oceans confirms this fact, and even shows this continental drift to be continuing today at the rate of about one inch per year. The May issue of *National Geographic* for 1975 carried an article on this very subject.

"There is no basis whatsoever for accepting the hypothesis that the earth consisted of but one continent *without hills and mountains* at the time of the flood. However, if, as has been suggested earlier, animals were created eons ago, it could certainly fit in with the concept of a primitive, one-continent condition as proposed by scientists. This would have provided opportunity for the created animals to have migrated to the distant parts of that continent, to be carried with those areas as they separated as a result of continental drift. Here then is additional proof of the eon 'day' concept of creation.

"One further word with regard to the length of the 'day' of Genesis. It is interesting that the Scripture tells us that God rested on the seventh day after the six days of creation. '. . . God rested on the seventh day . . . because in it He had rested from *all* the work which God *created* and *made*,' (Genesis 2:2 and 3). Now if the initial act of creation was not part of the six days, then God must have actually worked more than six days. To claim that this refers only to those things recorded from Genesis 1:2-27 is indeed working a travesty upon the truth of Scripture. To carry this thought still further, if the 'day' of Genesis was indeed a 24-hour period, then God must have *rested for only one day* from His work. Yet, there is no indication in Scripture or anywhere else that God has been working six days a week ever since. Instead, there is no indication anywhere that God has done any creative work (of a physical nature), since the original creative acts. The seventh day has already lasted for at least 6000 years.

"There are those who hold that there is confirmation of the 24-hour 'day' interpretation in the normal pattern of work for six days and rest for one. This pattern was established by God. Now assuming that the 'days' of Genesis were eons, God could certainly not expect man to work for six eons and rest for one. Instead, we see here simply a shadow or pattern of heavenly things. The Scripture abounds with examples, types, and patterns geared to man's ability, of which this is another."

CHAPTER VII

Creation

here is universal agreement among creationists that Genesis 1:1 refers to the initial act in which the universe was brought into existence out of nothing. The Scripture states that this was the result of God speaking. That's found in Psalm 33 Verse 6."

"Just a minute," Harry interrupted, "isn't that concept the main reason why Scientists reject the Scripture account? The belief that the universe was made from nothing? After all, we know that there are billions of galaxies in space, each containing billions of stars, and that the energy which this represents is so far beyond our comprehension, that it staggers the imagination. I know you said earlier that the universe is running down, and therefore must have had a beginning, but how could even God make the whole universe out of nothing?"

"That's a very good observation and question," answered Reverend Spangler. "I don't pretend to have all the answers either. I do not think that we will ever understand or comprehend the whole truth about creation this side of Heaven. But let me suggest something which has helped me in accepting, if not understanding the matter. I'm sure you have dreams, just as we all do. Haven't you noticed how absolutely real everything was in the dream? The place you were in, the people with whom you came in contact, the things that you did, weren't they just as solid, just as real as you experience while you are awake? I'm sure they were, yet, they did not exist at all except in your mind.

"Now I would like to take a certain amount of liberty with the Scripture, just for the purpose of trying to understand this whole matter of God creating everything from nothing.

"In Genesis 1:26 we read, 'Then God said, Let Us make Man in Our image, according to Our likeness . . .' Now let us suppose that God was saying, 'Let Us *imagine* a creature which We will call man. Let Us make him in such a way that he will have many of the same characteristics that We have.' Now, since God is a Spirit, not having a material body, but rather something which is completely foreign to our thinking, isn't it possible, that the very act of imagining, that is forming an image in the mind of God, would be all that was necessary to bring it into existence? We look at our universe, as you say, and are speechless at its wonders, expanse, and the enormous amount of energy represented. Yet, to God Who is above all and in all and through all, our universe may be but a very tiny thing relatively speaking. Our concept of the universe might be compared to that of an amoeba looking at the inside of your watch.

"Now, understand, I am not saying that this is the way it really is, but rather that thinking about it this way, might make it easier to understand. The apostle Paul stated it very well in the book of Romans Chapter 11 verses 33–36, where we read, 'Oh, the depth of the riches both of the wisdom and knowledge of God! How unsearchable are His judgements and unfathomable His ways! For who has known the mind of the Lord, or who became His counselor? Or who has first given to Him that it might be paid back to Him again? For from Him and through Him and to Him are all things. To Him be glory forever. Amen.'

"Now we come to an argument, (far fetched to be sure), which has been proposed to show that the earth has not existed for millions of years as claimed by science. This is the matter of death.''

"What has death got to do with the age of the earth, for goodness sake?" Jim asked.

"In my opinion, nothing," answered Reverend Spangler. "However, they point to the statement made in Romans 5:12, which states that death entered this world by means of the sin of Adam. Therefore, they claim, it would not have been possible for animals to have died prior to that time. Evidently these individuals overlooked the last part of this passage where the statement is made, '. . . and so death passed upon all men . . .' There is no reference to animals, and this is significant, since the Bible is very explicit in most cases, and the mere fact that this subject, death, is associated specifically with man, is highly important. We might even ask how animals sin, since the passage continues, 'for that all have sinned.' We can carry this thought even further and suggest that according to this theory, even grass, plants, and trees could not have died. Ridiculous? Well, let's examine this further.

"There are today, as there has been from at least the time of Adam, innumerable forms of bacteria, virus, noxious insects and other life forms. Now, if we take the position that *no* death occurred prior to the fall of man, we find ourselves in a serious dilemma. Either God created these after the fall, or they did not procreate prior to the fall. Simple logic and observation show that if insects were to continue to procreate without subsequent death, as by being eaten by birds, reptiles, etc., within an extremely short time, they would completely smother the surface of the earth.

"On the other hand, the Bible is very clear that God completed His creative work with the formation of man from the dust of the earth. 'In six days God created Heaven and earth and all that in them is.' Therefore, on Scriptural grounds, bacteria, virus, insects, and everything else must have been created prior to the fall, and thus, on practical grounds, these must have been subject to death, and therefore must have died, just as they do today.

"Even if we assume that *all* life forms were friendly to man prior to the fall, death of such forms must have been inevitable, just as it is today. I already mentioned vegetation in this regard, since vegetation, too, has life. Jesus Himself spoke of grain as dying when planted in the ground. Would not death of vegetation have occurred when eaten by animals as well as by man himself? Thus, we see that death, that is, physical death was a natural condition before the fall. However, in the case of man, physical death was something which could have been avoided by obedience to God's command. Note that Adam and Eve were expelled from the garden lest they eat of the tree of life and live forever.

"The whole problem in regard to the death judgement proclaimed against the human race is an understanding of the true meaning of the word 'death' as used in this connection. This word has two basic meanings, physical death or cessation of life, and spiritual death which is separation from God. Evidently, Adam and Eve were not surprised at God's command regarding the eating of the forbidden fruit. There is no reason to suppose that they asked God, 'What is death?' They were well aware of physical death, since they could observe it on every hand. Neither did Satan need to explain it to them. He spoke the truth, although only half, when he said, 'You surely shall not die.' And as we know, they did not die physically at that time, even though God had said, 'In the day thou eatest . . . thou shalt surely die.'

"Actually Adam and Eve had a choice, although they may not have realized it. Obedience to the command to abstain from eating the forbidden fruit would evidently have made them candidates to eat the fruit from the tree of life. Failure to obey would result in separation from God, and eventually in physical death as well. So the only reason for assuming that no death took place prior to the fall is to refute evolutionists or to refute those who hold to a very long, indeterminate age for the earth. I think you will agree that the facts I have just given take care of both of these cases.

"Now, you may wonder why I have spent so much time discussing the arguments concerning the length of days of

Genesis and the age of the earth. The fact is that both of these are essential to the theory of evolution, and therefore, if it could be shown that, either the days of creation were 24 hours duration each, or that the earth is only 10,000 to 12,000 years old, then the theory of evolution would be completely refuted." At this point, Harry spoke up and said, "Well, it seems to me that you have completely refuted the theories which have been put forth in both of those areas, but does that mean that you agree with the theory of evolution?"

"Absolutely not!" said Reverend Spangler. "You see, I take the Scriptures seriously, and where it speaks of searching to see if these things be true, I search. Too often we take someone else's word for something which may not present the true facts. Also, many things have been taken out of context to prove a point, and this is regrettable. In other cases, we may take a simple statement from the Bible, which by itself means one thing, but when taken with all of relevant Scripture, may be found to have a different connotation. For instance, when I was a boy, many Christians held to the belief that the world had to be flat, because the Scripture spoke of the four corners of the earth. Despite all the evidence, some still held to this belief because of the simple statement found in the Bible. Many years ago, it was heresy to claim that the earth was anything else but flat. The problem was that attention was not given to other parts of Scripture which refer to the earth as having a circle, and in another place as resting upon nothing. Taken all together, we see the earth as a sphere moving through space without support, but on which we find our direction by means of the four points, or corners, of the compass. Could there be a better way to indicate direction on a globe?

"So we see that the dogmatic position taken by well-meaning theologians has frequently been shown to be false, and not actually the true teaching of Scripture. This leads to mistrust on the part of unbelievers, and to a complete rejection of the story of creation by many Scientists."

"Reverend, a couple of sessions ago you referred to Creationists. Just who are they?" Harry asked.

"I guess I should have been more explicit," said the Reverend, "and qualified that term. Actually, anyone who accepts the teaching of Scripture, that God created the Heavens and the earth and everything on it, could be called a Creationist. However, there is a group, which as I have pointed out in these discussions, hold dogmatically to the 24-hour day theory, and usually also to the recent age for the earth. This is the group that I have been referring to as Creationists. On the other hand, there are many highly regarded scholars who believe in creation, but believe the days of creation were eons, and thus, ascribe a great age to the earth. Both of these groups refute the theory of evolution as commonly presented. Here again, there are diverse views on the subject of evolution. There are some, although few in number, who hold to a 'creative evolutionary theory.' According to this theory, God created the initial universe, including earth, and also created the first primitive life form. This then 'evolved,' mutated, and adapted to produce all the life forms that have ever inhabited the earth.

"Personally, I must reject this, if for no other reason than the fact that the Bible states that God created every life form. There are other reasons, too, which I will explain later. However, right now it is getting late, so we'll continue this next week at the same time."

CHAPTER VIII

The Primeval Earth

 arry Bolin and Jim Martin arrived promptly one week later. Reverend Spangler greeted them, and immediately started where he had left off the previous week.

"Before we discuss the relative merits of the theory of evolution versus Creation, I think we should consider just what evolution proposes. The term 'evolution' is itself simply a term to express the development leading to a definite end; an unfolding. We speak of the evolution of art, or the automobile. However, as it pertains to our present discussion, the reference is to the theory of the evolution or gradual progressive change from a simple life form to more and more, and more varied life forms through the process of adaptation, mutation, and selection. Most evolutionists also believe that the first life form to appear on the earth was spontaneously formed by chance as a result of certain natural forces acting on existing materials. We will discuss this later.

"As you can see from what I just said, there is a tremendous gulf between the theory of evolution and the story of creation as presented in Scripture. This becomes even greater if one insists on six, 24-hour days for Creation. At this point you may wonder if it is at all possible to reconcile these two points of view. I do not think so, since either God did in fact create the life forms on the earth, or they just happened by chance. I do not believe there is a middle ground. Either one accepts the Biblical account of Creation, or he accepts the theory of Evolution. Nevertheless, I feel that every theory should be studied as carefully as possible, looking at every relevant fact, and considering whether the deductions and reasoning used in arriving at the theory are logical and consistent.''

"Reverend," Jim said, "if the universe is billions of years old, and the earth is also very old, how does this fit in with the Creation account?" Reverend Spangler paused thoughtfully for a few moments, and then said, "I think we need to go back once again to the first few verses of the Genesis account, and see what is actually recorded there. Then without reading into it anything that is not implied, I believe we will get a better understanding of the entire event. Verse 2 of Genesis 1 states, 'And the earth was, (or became, or came into being), without form and void.' A little later, in Verse 5 of Chapter 2, we read that at that time there was not yet a shrub nor any plant. Also in Verse 2 of Chapter 1 we find that the water covered the surface of the earth. In other words, immediately after the initial Creation of our planet, it had no distinguishing features, and there was no life of any kind, vegetable or animal. The water covering the surface of the planet must have been very warm, saturating the atmosphere with moisture to such an extent that no light was able to penetrate to the surface. This is indicated in Genesis 1:2 and Genesis 2:6. After a period of time, this dense mist condensed so that light became visible. Land masses were raised above the surface of the sea, and the earth became suitable for vegetation. With the condensation of the dense mist, there was a separation between the surface of the planet and the clouds above. This is made very clear in Genesis 1:20, where we find the fowl of the air flying in the 'firmament' or 'open expanse of heaven,' found stated in the authorized and New American Standard translations respectively. When you stop and think about it, it is really amazing that the clouds do float a distance above the earth instead of close to the ground like a mist. Of course, we know that God ordained it so, and we can see and appreciate the advantages of such a system.

"Although the waters below the firmament were separated from those above, (clouds), it does not mean that the cloud layer was not extremely dense most of the time. However, in the light of Genesis 1:14, we must conclude that the sky was visible at times. Otherwise, how could the Heavenly bodies be used for signs and seasons? Despite this, the cloud layer must have been so dense most of the time, that there was a frequent misting taking place which watered the earth. We would conclude from these verses and others found in connection with the flood, that it did not rain, as we think of rain, prior to the flood, but rather there was a frequent and very likely heavy misting during this period. This would certainly help to explain the phenomenal growth and profusion of plant life that must have prevailed at one time in order to produce the fossil fuel deposits which were laid down during what is termed the carboniferous period."

At this point, Harry interrupted to ask a question. "Reverend, there are two points here that I can't seem to reconcile to the Creation account. I have heard that many scientists believe that the atmosphere of the earth consisted of methane and/or ammonia in its primeval form. If that is true, how could any form of life have survived, no less flourish under such conditions? In the second place, it is my understanding that Evolutionists claim that the first form of life was a simple cell, or amoeba-like life form. I believe they arrived at this conclusion as a result of certain experiments in which amino acids were formed when electrical discharges were passed through a mixture of gases, presumed to duplicate this primeval atmosphere."

"Those are very valid points," answered the Reverend, "and are questions that must be resolved if we are to understand the creation story in the light of all the available facts. Now, with regard to the primeval atmosphere, I do not agree at all with the position taken by Scientists that it consisted of methane and/ or ammonia, or anything like that. The primeval atmosphere could not have been a mixture of nitrogen and oxygen as it is today. But let us assume for a moment that the atmosphere was primarily methane and nitrogen. Let us further assume that by some unknown process, oxygen was gradually produced, to result in our present day atmosphere. Then, at one point in the process, the methane and oxygen would have reached critical proportions, at which time the smallest spark would have set off an explosion of gigantic proportions, enveloping the earth, and no doubt wiping out all life on it. An electrical storm or two stones striking each other would have been sufficient to do this.

"Secondly, as you already suggested, Harry, it would have been impossible for vegetable or animal life to have survived in such a proposed atmosphere. This is especially true of any form of animal life, which by the way, is the life form that is always suggested as the first form of life on the earth. Animal life is dependent on oxygen in one form or another, so it is completely unreasonable to assume that such could have survived, even if it had come into existence by some accidental, spontaneous process. Even if the first presumed life form was vegetable in nature and was able to survive and flourish in this unhospitable atmosphere, we are still faced with the problem of a critical mixture being formed as oxygen was released into the atmosphere. So, from every conceivable point of view, this theory is completely untenable. The principle reason for this proposal in the first place was to provide a basis for assuming that a freak accident had brought together the necessary raw materials to produce the first life form. Assuming that amino acids had been accidentally or spontaneously formed from the assumed atmosphere, and assuming further that somehow these had combined and polymerized to form protein, which eventually became a living cell, where would this cell have obtained the necessary food to survive? And, as we already mentioned, how could any life survive in such an atmosphere? Animal life is dependent upon vegetable life for its food supply, since only vegetable life can transform the chemicals that make up the atmosphere and soil into sources of energy. As you know, this is accomplished by photosynthesis, using the energy of the sun to bring about chemical processes which result in the formation of the needed organic chemicals. In the process, oxygen is released into the atmosphere or into water, and this oxygen is then used by animals to convert plant substances into energy. The by-product of this is carbon dioxide, which in turn is used by plants.

"In view of these facts, let us assume that the primeval atmosphere was a mixture of carbon dioxide and nitrogen. Let us further assume that the first life form on the earth was vegetable life, as the Bible states. In such an atmosphere, plant life would have grown at fantastic rates and very likely to enormous size. That this was actually the case is attested to by the extensive fossil fuel deposits of coal, within which are found the impressions of stems, leaves, and fronds of plants and ferns of great size, as well as of forms not living today. There are still enormous deposits of fossil fuels locked within the crust of the earth. Besides this, the earth is more or less covered with vegetation and animal life. It is an accepted fact that these fossil fuels are the direct result of an abundant plant and animal life which covered the earth at one time. Even if we accept the premise that crude oil originated with animal as well as vegetable life, we must still recognize that animal life was only possible as a result of vegetable life. Thus, all of the present day life, whether animal or vegetable, plus all the fossil fuels, represents an enormous amount of oxygen as having been released into the atmosphere at some time. Where did that oxygen come from? Certainly not from an atmosphere devoid of oxygen. Secondly, fossil fuels are basically carbon or carbon-rich compounds. Now, carbon is a very unreactive element. But it does react readily with oxygen at elevated temperatures. Science contends, and we have no reason to doubt this particular claim, that the earth originated in a very hot, probably molten condition, conditions ideal for carbon and oxygen to combine to form carbon dioxide.

"There is still further evidence to believe that the primeval atmosphere was carbon dioxide and nitrogen. In the earth's original molten or very hot condition, calcium carbonate, or limestone could not exist, since this decomposes readily at elevated temperature. Yet, today, there are enormous deposits, whole mountains as it were of limestone. Where did the carbon dioxide come from that combined with calcium to form this mineral? If, as I have suggested, the primeval atmosphere was indeed a mixture of carbon dioxide and nitrogen, this would easily explain the widespread occurrence of this common substance. This same process would also account for other minerals of a similar nature occurring as carbonates.

"In fact, there does not seem to be any alternative explanation. In passing, it is interesting to note that there are deposits in the earth of both native carbon and native sulfur. This suggests that the original reaction in which carbon combined with oxygen did not go to completion as there was not sufficient oxygen to combine with all the carbon and sulfur as well as other elements. I am not suggesting that what I have just proposed covers all the possible reactions which could and probably did take place in the earth and its atmosphere in the beginning. Many more elements and compounds were involved, as well as inter-reactions, double decompositions, and other chemical and physical reactions. What I am saying is, that in view of the present composition of the earth and its atmosphere, we may very logically assume that carbon dioxide and nitrogen were the principle components of the primeval atmosphere, and this in no way disagrees with the Biblical account. After all, the Biblical account does not say or even suggest the method or process by which God is said to have brought about the forming of the created material into the condition necessary for man to inhabit the earth. The earth as we see it today is far different from what it was at the time of the creation of man, and certainly before that. There is continual, gradual change taking place which we can see today, and which historically we have much evidence for. Therefore, we may logically assume that there was change taking place from the moment of the initial creation, which is certainly confirmed by the first several verses of Genesis 1."

CHAPTER IX

The First Life on Earth

volutionists hold to the position that the various life forms found on the earth today, as well as those that existed in the past, were the result of a gradual, progressive change beginning with a primitive single-celled creature, which in turn was the result of an accidental or spontaneous coalescence of protein and/or amino acids. As I mentioned in an earlier meeting, this very first block in the evolutionary building is found to be fantasy, especially since they invariably begin with animal life derived from the union of the necessary elements by pure chance to form these amino acids and protein. Besides rejecting the theory of evolution, and particularly the creation of the first life forms, for the reasons just given, there are also mathematical reasons based on the law of probabilities or chance. We were taught in school that the simplest life forms are single-celled creatures which are very simple in structure. Yet, we now know, that on the contrary, even a single-celled creature is enormously complex, and that the most baffling part of the single-celled creature is the ingredient of life. We can dissect the cell to a considerable degree; we can analyze it to determine its chemical components, but no one has yet found the most important ingredient of all—Life.

"In recent years we have had reports of the synthesis of 'living' substance being produced in the laboratory. Yet, even here, the starting materials were the product of some life form. Even more significant is the fact that this 'creation' was not the result of chance but the result of years of intensive, intelligent research, work, and direction. When we stop to consider that in contrast with this directed program, the spontaneous or accidental creation of the first single-celled creature, according to the evolutionary concept, would have been the result of the chance union of sterile, inorganic elements and compounds, we see the utter impossibility of the theory. Even a single cell, according to this theory, would have been the result of the accidental union of six of the nearly one hundred elements in nature, in the right proportion, in the right sequence, at the right time, at the right place; and at the same time omitting all other elements. At this point someone will say that only the right elements were present since the reaction probably took place in the atmosphere where only hydrogen, nitrogen, and oxygen were present in quantity, with just enough of the other necessary elements. Thus, it would require only the proper conditions of electrical discharge or actinic radiation to bring about the reactions necessary for the formation of protein material. We might even go so far, for the sake of argument, to grant such a possibility, but let us consider the fact that a single cell contains not just one molecule of protein, or for that matter only one kind of protein, but rather, millions of molecules of protein of many different chemical compositions. Furthermore, these molecules, (assuming that they were all present), would need to be brought together in the right sequence and the right proportions, under the proper conditions and in the right place. And, it would still be a dead cell, assuming of course, that this had all taken place in such a way as to enclose itself in a cell wall or sac. Then, assuming still further, that such had happened, and that somehow it had attained life, it would still have had to have the ability to find and utilize food; to reproduce itself; and to have had the potential of becoming more and more complex and of adapting to its environment, even when such meant a change in size, mobility and nature.

"Charles Eugene Guye calculated the probability of the spontaneous or accidental creation of a single *protein* molecule as happening once in 10^{243} years. That is millions of billions of years for the possible formation of *one* protein molecule. Some calculations have also been made relative to the probabilities of the evolution of a relatively simple life form, assuming that a single-celled creature already existed. We are speaking now of a life form having 200 integrated functioning parts. This would still be a very simple life form, yet, even in such an organism, the chances for it to have been formed by the successive, successful mutations, just once, anywhere in the world, in all the expanse of geologic time, is less than one chance out of a billion trillion.

"Now if we combine these two mathematical probabilities— the formation of the first protein molecule and the combining of this with other protein molecules followed by mutation and natural selection to produce a simple life form, we arrive at a figure which defies the imagination.

"In a paper presented at a meeting of the American Association for the Advancement of Science, it was pointed out that Darwin's theory of evolution has failed another test. If his theory were true, there would be an increase in the number of chromosomes and the quality of gene material carried by the chromosomes as the complexity of animals increased. Actually this was not the case, and in fact, chromosome counts showed man ranking lower than frogs and toads. It was then suggested that there were probably many spontaneous beginnings of life on earth. It should be obvious to the reader that this would increase the odds even higher for the possibility of spontaneous creation of life.

"The same paper included the statement that there also was no scientific link between major kinds of plants, and that the study on which this was based had not shown any connection between plants and animals. This truth was expressed in the

Bible thousands of year ago, where we read, '. . . let the earth bring forth grass, the herb yielding seed, and the fruit tree yielding fruit after his kind . . .' Also, '. . . let the earth bring forth the living creature after his kind. . .' (Genesis 1:11 and 24).

"Every consideration given to the subject of evolution must of necessity be based on the assumption that matter, as represented by the atoms and molecules of which the earth is composed, was already in existence before any spontaneous or accidental formation of amino acid or protein could take place. This of course, brings us back to the question of the origin of matter, and it would seem appropriate therefore, to consider the building blocks of which matter is composed—the atoms.

"The atom is composed, like a miniature solar system, of a nucleus carrying a positive charge of electricity, and electrons orbiting the nucleus with a negative charge of electricity. It has been estimated that electrons travel around the nucleus billions of times each millionth of a second. This is only possible because of the unlike charges which attract each other. Furthermore, the nucleus consists of protons with a positive charge and neutrons with no charge. The mystery is why the protons do not repel each other and scatter into space. Some force, not yet known, causes these to remain within the nucleus, thus, providing the positive charge which holds the electrons in orbit. While the mathematical properties of this binding force have been determined, we still do not know what it is or how it came into being. That is, we do not know unless we accept the Biblical statement, '. . . for by Him were all things created . . . and by Him all things consist, (are held together).' Einstein, in his theory of relativity, proposed a formula showing that all matter is really energy and may be represented by the equation $E = MC^2$. Subsequent experiments have demonstrated the truth of the theory, a by-product of which was the atomic bomb and nuclear energy.

"With further reference to the neutrons within the nucleus of the atom, when these are smashed, they become electrons, protons and a multitude of other particles which completely baffle the scientists. Altogether, we are just beginning to appreciate the vast amount of energy stored within the atom, and we must stand in awe as we realize that every speck of matter, visible and invisible, is a storehouse of unbelievable energy, held in perfect control by a force which is beyond comprehension. At this point even the most dogmatic evolutionist must admit to ignorance or accept the creationist's view as outlined in Scripture."

CHAPTER X

Darwin's Theory of Evolution

fter a short pause, Reverend Spangler continued. "Now, since science takes the position that the Bible is not a true account of the origin of the universe, we might ask, what they consider it to be. Actually, there are many scientists who do accept the Bible as the inspired word of God, but these are in the minority. The majority, who are not familiar with the Bible, but only know what they hear, consider it as an attempt to attribute those things which cannot be explained by other means, to an unseen, imaginary, Supreme Being. Even more unfortunate is the fact that theologians, Bible scholars, and lecturers have propounded their private interpretations of Scriptural accounts, and as we have already shown, these are frequently neither Scriptural nor logically sound. Other scientists accept the doctrine of a special, initial, creative act, including the first life form, but credit the evolutionary process with the rest.

"As we noted earlier, the Bible credits God with the Creation of the Heavens and the earth at the very beginning. It is also interesting that the book of Job, which is believed by many to antedate the book of Genesis, confirms this. Of even greater significance is the confirmation given by Jesus Himself as recorded in the book of Mark. '. . . from the beginning of the creation, God made them male and female. . .' (Mark 10:6). Also, '. . . from the beginning of the creation which God Created. . .' (Mark 13:19). The apostle John, in writing the book of Revelation, also refers to this Creative act. '. . . Him that liveth for ever and ever, Who Created Heaven, and the things that therein are. . .' (Revelation 10:6). In still another place he writes, '. . . O, Lord . . . Thou hast Created all things. . .' (Revelation 4:11). It should be noted first of all from these passages that only one Creation is mentioned. There was no original Creation destroyed by God and then a new Creation. Secondly, according to Mark, God made them male and female. This is shown also in Genesis 5:2 where it says, '. . .in the day that God Created them.' Now, since woman was not 'made' until after the sixth day, we have a problem, since God is said to have rested from all His work (Genesis 2:2). Some may say that actually, Eve was Created in Adam since God took one of Adam's ribs to make Eve. This does not follow the references already given, where *they* were both made, and stipulated to be male and female. There appears to be but one explanation, and that is that the 'days' of Genesis cannot be restricted to 24-hour periods, and as far as God is concerned, He did not complete His work until after Eve had been brought on the scene. Thirdly, we notice from the passages cited above that the creative work was a continuing process, since the Creations began 'in the beginning,' or 'from the beginning.' So again, we have conclusive proof that the Genesis account represents a continuing process of succeeding acts without interruption.

"Because scientists, by and large, have rejected the doctrines proposed by Creationists, which as we have shown are not always Scriptural, the Creationists have in turn rejected most of the theories proposed by Science to explain the origin of the universe and life. The primary theory to which Creationists object, of course, is the theory of evolution, and unfortunately these people have proposed several untenable theories of their own to refute the theory of evolution.

"Darwin proposed, as did others, that all life forms have a common ancestor, and that due to mutation, changes in environment and food supply, new life forms came into existence of a more and more complex nature, with ability to adapt to their environment. At the same time, less adaptable life forms gradually disappeared.

"It is very significant that Paleontologists have found that most new life forms represented by fossil remains appeared suddenly on the scene. That is, there was no very gradual development and proliferation of new life forms, as the Darwinian theory of evolution proposes. Instead, there are suddenly, (geologically speaking), numerous examples of the new life forms. This is of course exactly what the Scripture states took place. Another highly significant fact is that there are living today, many life forms which are to all intent and purposes identical to some which lived millions of years ago, and whose fossil remains have been found. Now, this presents a problem for the Evolutionists. If changing environment demanded a change in the life form, why didn't these present day examples also adapt? On the other hand, if it was not necessary to change to adapt to new conditions, why did some change? We know that animals can and do change their appearance, shape or size within certain limits when the environment demands it. We can see examples of this today. Extensive experiments have been conducted, using bacteria and insects having rapid reproduction cycles, in an effort to produce a mutation or new life form that would be substantially different from the parent. Some mutations have been produced, but nothing substantially different, and certainly nothing that could be considered a transmutation as the theory of evolution proposes. It is also significant that in many of these cases the mutants were sterile. To date, there is no evidence that sufficient changes have ever taken place in any life form to confirm the Darwinian theory of evolution. The examples given by Evolutionists, such as that of the horse, have been shown to be completely in error. And even if we could accept this example as fact, it in no way satisfies the requirements for transmutation, or change from one specie to another, from fish to fowl, or from reptile to mammal.

"As I mentioned earlier, the Evolutionists have taken the observed minor changes of adaptation and applied them to the unsubstantiated, highly improbable, and we might even say impossible, changes needed to support the theory of evolution. The time required to permit even one significant mutation or change of specie has been estimated to be more than the estimated age of the earth, which fact is enough by itself to refute this theory."

Again Harry spoke up. "But Reverend, doesn't the geologic column substantiate the theory of Evolution? After all, it does show simple life forms in the lowest, oldest levels, with more and more complex forms as time progressed."

"The sequence of life forms from simpler to more complex forms is, of course, an observed fact," answered Reverend Spangler. "However, this is also the substance of the Biblical account. Also, as I already mentioned, Paleontology has shown that in accordance with the Biblical account, new life forms appeared suddenly, not very gradually as the theory of evolution proposes."

Now Jim asked a question. "Pastor, does the theory of evolution suggest that every individual in a particular life form changed or mutated at the same time?"

"Actually," answered Reverend Spangler, "this is one detail that is not stressed by the Evolutionists. One infers that only one individual mutated or changed enough to be termed different from its parent. This, of course, presents another very serious problem, since if this were the case, there would not be another similar mutant with which to mate, and therefore there would be an assimilation of the 'new' form back into the basic form. This principle is still active today."

"Could you give us an illustration?" asked Jim.

"Certainly. I'm sure you are familiar with the practice of grafting of fruit trees, shrubs, and vines. At some time, a 'sport' developed on a tree or shrub or vine which produced fruit or flowers of a more desirable color, taste or appearance. When seeds from these fruits or flowers are planted, the resulting plant does not produce the new variety, but rather the same as the original plant, or perhaps something even different.

"To obtain the new variety, it is necessary to graft a stem or bud which produces the new variety onto another plant. The graft then grows and continues to produce the new variety. Left to natural processes, there will not be a continued propagation of the new variety once the grafted plant dies. Also, it is significant that seeds from these mutants are often less able to continue to propagate. Hybrid grains are another example. These must be developed and grown by special means. If left to themselves, they will revert to the original type. This is also true in the animal world, where breeding of livestock and pets must be carefully controlled or the strain will revert to an ancestral type. It has been found that there is a limit in all of these breeding processes to which the upgrading can be carried. And we must remember that this is done under carefully controlled, sophisticated methods. To assume that under natural conditions this process would proceed and result in more and more complex and varied life forms is completely illogical."

"Well, then," Harry asked, "in view of the lack of evidence for the theory of evolution, just what do they base their theory on?"

"As I suggested earlier," the Reverend said, "it is based largely on the observed fact of adaptation. Also, an integral part of the theory is that of survival of the fittest. This is something we can observe and accept today. For instance, a carnivore will attack and kill the weak members of a herd of deer. The stronger, faster, or wiser individuals escape. Based on the theory of evolution we would expect deer to 'develop' or 'evolve' with wings so as to more easily escape. Again, we must emphasize that there is no evidence to suggest that this ever happened with any life form."

Jim spoke up again. "Wouldn't such a change necessarily need to take place suddenly if conditions were not satisfactory for continued survival?"

"That is true," said Reverend Spangler, "as is the fact that if conditions were satisfactory, no change would be needed. Let us imagine that due to a sudden shift in the earth's crust, climatic conditions became unsuitable for certain life forms. They would need to change drastically within a short period of time or they would be exterminated. On the other hand, if those changes were not sufficient to exterminate them in the form in which they then existed, why would they need to change? A good example of this is the frozen remains of wooley mammoths found in Siberia and other places. Some catastrophic event undoubtedly occurred while they were grazing on vegetation, causing them to be frozen with grass still in their mouths. They would not have been killed if they had been able to withstand these changed conditions.

"It is also interesting to note that there are a number of animal specie living today which have adapted to their environment with practically no change in appearance or form. The coyote lives in forested areas, plains, and in the desert. Its eating habits reflect the available food supply, yet the coyote appears virtually the same in whatever environment it lives. This same truth applies to many other animals as well. So we come back to our original statement that if environmental changes required basic changes in the life form, that life form would have expired. Conversely, if no change was needed to adapt to the changed conditions, why would any have occurred? There are living today, numerous life forms which are practically identical to fossil remains, millions of years old. If these life forms were able to exist without change, why did others find it necessary to change under conditions which obviously had not changed substantially during that period of time?

"We have now come full circle, as it were, to our reason for these meetings, namely the finding of a fossil claimed to be that of the missing link. To begin with, this term is used in the sense of being the life form intermediate between the 'ape-men' and true man. The similarities between apes, monkeys, and other members of that group, and man, are very obvious. This has led to the postulation that man and apes are descended from a common ancestor. It is this common ancestor which is often termed the 'missing link.' However, there are also many 'missing links' in the various phylum or groups of animals assumed to have a common ancestor. The main problem we are faced with here is as we have just discussed, the reason for a change of major proportions. While it is true there are many similarities between members of these groups, there are also many dissimilarities. We could liken this to the similarities between all the brands of cars, or between the various models of one particular manufacturer. The models are similar because one company makes them. Following this reasoning, there are similarities to be expected in the things that our Creator made. Ford cars did not evolve into Cadillacs, or Lincolns from Plymouths.

"Now with regard to this latest find, again we need to note that it is not a human fossil. It is man-like in many respects, but not human, and certainly not a 'missing link.' If this were the case, then the apes, which also had descended from this so-called common ancestor, would then be not higher or more complex than its ancestor, but rather lower, which is the opposite of what evolution teaches.

"Well, I think we have talked long enough for one night, so I think we better cut our discussions off now and resume them next week," said Reverend Spangler.

"The time seems to go by fast, I can hardly believe it is so late," said Jim. Harry echoed this remark, and then they both departed for their homes.

CHAPTER XI

The Missing Link

ood evening." Reverend Spangler greeted his guests a week later. "Please come in."

"Reverend," Harry began, "I have been thinking about last week's discussion regarding the 'missing link,' and I talked to a friend of mine one day about our talks. He made a very interesting statement that I would like you to comment on, if you will." "I'd be more than happy to if I can," answered the Reverend. "Well," Harry continued, "he suggested the possibility that at some point early in man's history, while he was still living a very primitive life, he mated with man-like creatures, which resulted in off-spring which produced the fossil remains that today baffle the paleontologists and gives a basis for the 'missing link' theory. I have never heard this before, and I know of nothing to support this idea. What do you think?" "That's a new one to me," answered Reverend Spangler, "but you know it does have some merit, when one stops to think about it. In the sixth chapter of Genesis, a situation is described that has puzzled theologians for a very long time. It reads as follows, '. . . when men began to multiply . . . and daughters were born to them . . . the sons of God saw that the daughters of men were beautiful, they took wives for themselves, whomever they chose.' (A.R.S.). Some believe this refers to sons of Seth as sons of God, marrying daughters of Cain. There are two problems associated with this theory. First, why would this union result in giants? Secondly, what about the union of daughters of Seth and sons of Cain? Would they not have also married? The other, more widely accepted view is that this account refers to angelic beings cohabiting with mortal women. This also presents a serious problem in that angelic beings are stated to be sexless, or at least do not marry nor are given in marriage. (Matthew 22:30). Again, there is the question as to why this would result in giants. Some have contended that the mythological gods and goddesses of Greece, Rome, and other peoples were in fact these angelic beings, and that the intermarriage of these with humans is the same as the Genesis account. A passage in Jude, Verse 6, is sometimes used to confirm this intermarriage of angelic beings with humans, but a careful study of that passage would seem to rule out any such thought.

"But getting back to the Genesis account in Chapter 6, I can see where this could possibly have referred, not to either of the two theories I just mentioned, but rather to the intermarriage of humans, 'sons of God,' since they were especially created in the image of God, and man-like animals. Perverted men even today mate with animals, such as sheep, dogs, and cattle. So it is not difficult to believe that this act or acts was such an abomination to God that it brought about the judgement, recorded in the account of the flood."

"But wait a minute," Jim said, "the Bible suggests that Adam and Eve were created only some 6,000 years ago. How could the 'missing link' fossils fit into that theory? They are dated at several times that age." "Well, let's look at the facts, both observed and inferred," said Reverend Spangler. "In the first place, I am not convinced that the so-called 'missing link' is a representative of this theoretical union, but may rather be a representative of the man-like animals with which this union might have taken place. Secondly, there have been severe doubts about the age of many, if not all, of the fossil remains that have been found to date. In fact, some have been labeled as outright frauds. In the third place, we have no way of knowing how many years ago Adam and Eve walked this earth. There are, as you know, many gaps in the geneologies of the Bible. The expression, 'begat' for instance, does not necessarily mean an immediate child, but could refer to a great, great grandchild. Likewise, 'father' often refers to a great, great grandfather for example. The geneologies given were for the purpose of providing a basis for ancestry, not necessarily complete to the extent that they included every single individual in the line. Therefore, Adam and Eve could have lived much more than 6,000 years ago. Some have suggested 10,000 years, and some have suggested much longer than that. This is somewhat born out by the extent and size of the population we find in the early chapters of Genesis.

"Another item of interest is in connection with the source of wives for sons of Adam and Eve. Most Bible scholars suggest that they married their sisters, but there is no evidence for this. The point is, that the sixth chapter of Genesis could refer to the unholy union of true men with man-like creatures, and thus, brought about the flood judgement. However, again we have no evidence to substantiate this theory, and so we can only say that it is interesting, and possibly inferred from the book of Genesis.

"There is another theory that has been suggested also to explain the so-called 'missing links' or more properly, man-like creatures such as the Neanderthal Man and the Piltdown Man. Throughout the history of man there have been instances of 'throwbacks' or mutants of human beings which have appeared more animalistic than human. Even today there are examples of this. The skulls of certain individuals could easily be mistaken for that of a member of the ape family. Others have distorted features, deformed bodies, and other abnormalities. Now, it is a generally well accepted fact that ancient peoples, in particular, thought that anyone who appeared abnormal should be driven out of the tribe and ostracized from society. This has led to the suggestion that the fossil remains of these man-like creatures were in fact abnormal individuals who had been driven from their tribe and found refuge in caves or other places where they lived out their lives in more or less seclusion. This would also explain why these man-like creatures' remains are associated with fire and remains of animals used for food. Frankly, I am inclined much more to this theory than to any other."

"Well, that settles it as far as I am concerned," said Jim. "I had no idea you had made such a study of this matter of Creation and Evolution."

"I found it necessary to do so," said Reverend Spangler, "since this comes up periodically every time some Scientist makes an announcement that he has discovered the 'missing link' or has been able to synthesize living protein from inert material, or some other 'discovery' that refutes the Bible. I am always amazed that with all our knowledge and skill, the Bible has still never been shown to be false in even one respect. This alone should be enough to assure us that the Bible is in fact the word of God and can be relied on completely."

Now Harry added his voice to the discussion. "I'm in full agreement with Jim, Reverend Spangler. I must admit I have had doubts from time to time in the light of these so-called discoveries and theories about the beginning of life on earth. Being a chemist, I can wholeheartedly agree with your arguments about the composition of the earth's primeval atmosphere. I don't see how they could have overlooked the fact that if it had been methane, there would have come a time when the oxygen-methane ratio reached a critical point and there would inevitably have been a worldwide explosion, the likes of which had never been seen. I can certainly agree with you that this would have wiped out all life on the earth. I also agree with you that no life of any kind could have lived and propagated in such a hostile atmosphere. It seems to me that some so-called scientists have gone to great extremes to prove the Scriptural account of Creation false. I like that theory about the origin of the fossils of man-like creatures that have been linked to man. I have read about aboriginal tribes living today that will not tolerate abnormal-looking individuals in their midst. Some nationalities within recent years even destroyed twins when born, fearing some evil.

I can certainly see where primitive tribes would have driven abnormal humans from the tribe, either to preserve the stock or because of superstitions."

"Thanks for your expressions of confidence in me," said the Reverend. "One thing that I trust I will never be accused of, is being dogmatic. I admit that there are some things about which I am thoroughly convinced, and about which I can be dogmatic on Scriptural grounds. But where the Bible is not absolutely clear, I am perfectly willing to consider various interpretations. The thing that has bothered me most in recent years is not so much the theory of evolution and the various ramifications, such as the composition of the primeval atmosphere, but the far-fetched counter theories proposed by well-meaning theologians and Bible scholars, particularly when there is no Scriptural basis for them, or when they take passages out of context. After all, as Christians, we should handle the word of God honestly and reverently. Another thing that has bothered me is the extent to which some of these individuals have gone to define certain words in the Bible. I mentioned several of these earlier in our talks.

"I trust that these discussions have been helpful to you, and I do want to thank you for your patience. It has really been very enjoyable for me to take this time to talk about these subjects."

"Pastor," Jim said, "I've enjoyed these talks tremendously, and hate to see them come to an end. Couldn't we continue these sessions, perhaps discussing some of the other controversial subjects? Personally, I'd like to hear what you have to say about the flood. I know that there are two views as to the extent, some saying it was local and others worldwide, among other aspects. Couldn't we continue these meetings?"

Harry then added his voice to Jim's plea. "I'd sure like to have you continue with these meetings, too. I'm especially interested in the account of the flood. There are some views on this subject that are a little hard for me to swallow. I'd sure appreciate it if you would consent to continue these weekly get-togethers."

"I was afraid maybe you were getting tired of coming out every week to hear me talk," said the Reverend, "but if you want to continue, that's fine with me. We'll plan on next week, same time then."

"That's mighty nice of you," said Jim. "We'll be here. Thanks again, and good night."

"That goes for me, too," said Harry. "Good night."

CHAPTER XII

The Flood

 week later, the three men were once more seated in the Reverend Spangler's living room. After usual salutations, he said, "Friends, you asked me to discuss the subject of the flood, so let's get right into it. You will recall that several weeks ago, in talking about the condition of the earth in its primeval form, before there was life of any kind, I spoke of the heavy mist which covered the surface. It seems perfectly clear to me, from the Genesis account, that there came a time when this mist broke causing a separation between the earth's surface and the heavy cloud layer above. The authorized version of the Bible uses the word firmament in connection with this. We see this simply as the air space between the surface and the clouds. Birds are recorded as flying in this 'firmament,' that is the air space above the earth.

"It seems entirely logical to me that while there was now an air space between the surface of the earth and the cloud layer above, this cloud layer must have still been extremely dense. Furthermore, as confirmed by the Biblical account, this cloud layer must have been so dense that a fine mist filtered down at frequent intervals, 'watering the earth.' Now, you might ask, 'what has that got to do with the flood?'

"One of the questions concerning the flood has always been, 'where did all the water come from to completely cover the entire earth, including the high mountains?' In order to answer this, some have suggested that the dense cloud layer I have just described was in effect a vapor canopy. Then, the flood waters were the result of this 'vapor canopy' condensing into torrential rain. Now, before looking at the various arguments pro and con to this theory, we should note that the tradition of a great deluge is widespread throughout the world. Details of these accounts vary widely, and some may in fact be exaggerations of some local disaster. Still, it is difficult to believe that so many diverse peoples, scattered over the face of the earth, could all have arrived at such a remarkable coincidence of outline, unless there had indeed been a worldwide catastrophe, or a common tradition handed down from one generation to the next.

"Many, if not all scientists, agree that there is overwhelming evidence to support belief that the earth has been subjected to one, and probably more than one, catastrophic event. Even the asteroid belt in our solar system suggests that at some time in the distant past, a planet, perhaps similar to earth, orbited the sun in the approximate location of the asteroids. Some have suggested that this planet either exploded, or more likely, disintegrated as the result of a collision with another heavenly body. If such were actually the case, it would explain in part the dislocation of great blocks of the earth's crust, and other geologic evidence indicating tremendous stresses in the earth's crust. Some writers have suggested that the earth has been subjected to a number of catastrophic events, the most recent being the flood recorded in the book of Genesis. Causes for this flood have been described as having been the result of the condensation of the 'vapor canopy,' or by the approach of a heavenly body, causing tremendous tidal waves, collapse of an ice canopy, or other catastrophic event. Whatever the cause, we have every reason to believe that there was indeed at some time in the not too distant past a flood which covered part, if not all, of the earth's surface.

"Now, getting back to the various reasons or causes for the flood, we note that Creationists, for the most part, attribute the flood to an act of God, without giving any scientific explanation whatsoever. Now let me hasten to say that I am convinced that God was indeed the Author of the flood. This does not mean that He did not use natural forces to bring it about. However, we should note that there is no indication of a creative act in bringing water into existence to produce the flood; that is, water which had not already been created. Furthermore, there is no suggestion of a destruction of water, (un-creation), if you please, in order to restore the earth to its former condition. One thing is very clear: the water which 'covered the earth' came from rain and from the sea, 'fountains of the deep.' A second fact, which many have seemingly overlooked, is the statement in Genesis 8:3 that, '. . . the waters *returned* from off the earth continually . . .' This is followed in the eighth verse by the statement, '. . . to see if the waters were *abated* from off the face of the ground . . .' Now, what does this imply? Simply that the flood was not a worldwide, but rather a local catastrophe. Now, before you raise your questions about that statement, let me hasten to say that this is one of the principal points on which theologians differ. Most do hold that the flood was worldwide, and that this is proven by Scripture which states that 'all the high mountains . . . were covered.' Now I will grant that this seems to be completely contradictory. Either the earth was completely covered, or the Bible is in error. Since we believe the Bible in its original text was without error, how can we reconcile these two opposite positions?

"First of all, I think we need to recognize that when the word translated 'all' is used, it does not necessarily mean, 'nothing excluded.' Rather, it means all in relation to the specific subject or area involved. A very simple example of this is found in connection with the flood account. In Genesis 6:13 we read: 'The end of *all* flesh is come before me . . . I am about to destroy them with the earth.' Now, 'all flesh' would have included Noah and his family. Did God in fact destroy them? No, and in fact

He did not destroy the earth either. Now are we to conclude that God lied, or didn't mean what He said? I can't go along with that. In an earlier verse we read: 'I will blot out man.' Thus, the 'all' referred to the wicked men, that is, all who did not recognize and honor the Creator. There are other instances also where the word 'all' has reference to all within the specific subject area. In the case of the flood, 'all' could have had reference to the inhabited portion of the earth. One might even ask, 'why would the entire earth need to be covered to a depth of five miles with water, in order to destroy those living within a limited area?' "

At this point, Jim could no longer contain himself. "Pastor," he asked, "isn't there anything else in Scripture that has a bearing on this matter?"

"Fortunately there is," answered Reverend Spangler. "There is a passage in II Peter, Chapter 3, verses 5 and 6, which is quite specific. Peter is speaking of the destruction that resulted from the flood. He is not speaking about the primeval earth. Thus we read, '. . . by the word of God the Heavens were of old, and the earth standing out of the water and in the water: whereby the world that then was, being overflowed with water, perished . . .' Two important statements are contained in these verses that are pertinent to this discussion. First, the earth is stated to be standing out of the water and in the water. This does not depict a universal flood. Secondly, the *world* was overflowed, speaks first of all of a world system or mankind, and secondly, this is what was overflowed, not submerged, as would have been the case of a worldwide flood. This then would explain why it was not necessary for God to create sufficient water to cover the entire earth to a depth of five miles in order to cover all the mountains. It would also be far more rational than to cover the entire earth in order to destroy those within a rather limited area of the earth's surface, the 'world' of that day.

"A little while ago I mentioned the Scripture which speaks of the water returning off the earth, and abating from the face of the earth. When we consider these in the light of the statement in II Peter which I just quoted, I think we have a very clear picture of a localized flood. On the other hand, if we were to be dogmatic about the worldwide nature of the flood, we are faced with some very serious questions. First, how could water return off the earth if the entire earth was covered with water? Where would it go? Now, some claim that since the water came by an act of God, it could be removed in a similar fashion. Once again, we would have to admit that with God nothing is impossible. In this case however, there is no indication that He did indeed miraculously cause the water to disappear. Rather, it returned from off the earth, obviously referring to the sea, since the statement is made that it came originally from rain *and* the fountains of the deep. Reference to abating from off the earth suggests the same phenomena.

"The torrential rains certainly could have been condensation of the dense cloud layer, and the fountains of the deep could certainly have been the seas leaving their basins to cover the world of that day. But as to the cause of this, we can only conjecture. But, before doing that, I think we should also look at the theory known as the 'ice canopy' theory. This is based entirely on the statement made in Genesis 1, verses 6 and 7, where we read, 'God said, "let there be a firmament between the waters to divide waters from waters;" so God made the firmament and separated the waters under the firmament from the waters above the firmament.' The theory continues with the assumption that the firmament is the atmosphere, and therefore, the waters above the firmament were actually above the atmosphere, or about one hundred miles above the earth's surface. Also, since it is so cold at that altitude, the water would of necessity be ice, thus, an ice canopy. This ice canopy is pictured as a hollow sphere completely enclosing the earth, but only about one foot thick. Since this canopy would be roughly 26,000 miles in circumference, it would be the flimsiest ball that one could imagine. The same author of this theory attributes the flood to the disintegration and melting of this hollow ball of ice. A simple calculation will show that such an ice canopy would have had to have been *five miles* thick to provide the water necessary to completely cover the highest mountains on earth, assuming it was of a worldwide nature. To overcome this problem, it was assumed that there were no mountains or hills on the earth at that time. This is, of course, in complete contradiction to the Genesis account."

"How could anyone come up with such a hair-brained theory?" asked Harry.

"Well," said Jim, "I suppose when you are trying to prove your position, you will grasp at anything to support it. Still, I don't see how they could have been a student of the Bible and propose anything as contradictory as that."

"Yes, as you say, gentlemen," Reverend Spangler said, "once a person is committed to a dogmatic position, he will do anything to support it. But, let's carry on where we left off.

"The question still remains as to how a local flood could have occurred and how it could have been of such a magnitude, assuming that it was in fact local. I have to admit that there are too many unanswered questions for me to be dogmatic about this either. I am convinced that there was a flood; that Noah did build an ark; and that remains of the ark are still on Mt. Ararat. The evidence concerning this last point is quite overwhelming in my opinion.

"Several weeks ago, I mentioned that in connection with a TV presentation of a documentary on the ark, an astronomer had been interviewed, who said that an extraterrestrial body coming into close proximity to the earth could have drawn the seas from their basins. We are, of course, well aware of the effect of the gravitational pull of the sun and the moon on our oceans to produce the tides. The same phenomena on a much larger scale could be attributed to such an approach by some interstellar body.

"Some years ago, I read somewhere that someone had suggested that the flood may have been caused by the close approach of a meteor which is, of course, the same idea. Now it is very interesting that meteors have been described as 'dirty snowballs.' In other words, they are primarily ice. However, in order for such a visitor from space to cause a local flood such as described in the Genesis account, this foreign body would, of necessity, need to remain in orbit around the earth, traveling at the same speed, relatively speaking, as the earth's surface, so that it would remain over one specific area for a prolonged period of time. The possibility of this has been demonstrated, of course, in recent years with the orbiting of man-made satellites. I consulted with two astronomers on the possibilities of such an event, and both of them, unknown to each other, confirmed the theoretical possibility of such a situation. However, they both agreed that for such a thing to take place, a third body would be required to absorb the energy of its speed, in order to slow it sufficiently to take up such an apparently fixed position above the earth. One possibility is that our moon was that third body. Some support to such a theory is found in Scripture. In the first chapter of Genesis, two lights are said to have been made, one to rule the day, and one to rule the night. Now, we know that the moon at present does not rule the night except for a few days each month, thus suggesting that the period of rotation around the earth has been changed. Many astronomers believe that some, if not all, of the moons of Jupiter are captive moons, thus lending strength to the possibility of a captive meteor. The close proximity of such an extraterrestrial body would certainly cause torrential rains and tidal movement, all of which fits the description given in the Bible.

"Now, to examine this theory further, let us assume that an ice comet did, in fact, take up a more or less fixed orbit above the earth in the vicinity of Turkey and the Arabian peninsula. First of all, there would be tidal inundation as the seas were drawn from their basins due to the gravitational pull of the comet. Secondly, there would be torrential rains as the thick cloud layer condensed. Then gradually, the comet would be drawn closer and closer causing it to disintegrate, raining ice upon the earth, which in that warm climate would melt into more and more rain. No doubt there would be rain and ice falling over a much larger area of the earth as well, but where the ice fell in arctic regions it would not melt. Since this would be extremely cold, it would have killed and quick frozen any animals living there. It may be significant that in recent years, great woolly mammoths have been found, still buried in ice, some with food still in their mouths, indicating instant death. The flesh of these animals has been preserved in excellent condition to this day, attesting to the rapid manner in which they had been frozen. No suitable explanation has been found to explain this condition, unless the concept of the ice comet is in fact tenable.

"To expand this theory still further, two scientific facts may be cited. One is that the ice age(s) has never been satisfactorily explained. Many scientists hold that the earth went through a period, or periods, of alternating warm and cold cycles causing an advance and receding of the polar ice caps. The reason given for these changes is an increase or decrease in the amount of carbon dioxide in the atmosphere. We do have evidence that at one time the polar regions were temperate or subtropical in climate. Fossils and deposits of fossil fuels attest to that fact.

"The Scriptural description of the early life on earth seems to agree with this, and such a condition would be logical, assuming that a very heavy cloud layer or vapor canopy surrounded the earth prior to the flood. Now, if an ice comet did indeed come in close proximity to the earth, and eventually disintegrated and fell to the surface as ice and rain, a condition similar, if not identical to that of an ice age would surely have resulted.

"Most people are more or less familiar with the geologic formation known as the continental shelves. This is an area of varying width surrounding most of the continents of the earth, and lying at depths averaging 200 feet below sea level. The only explanation for these shelves has been that the sea level rose following the last ice age as a result of the receding, melting ice caps. The trouble with this hypothesis is that the seas must also have been more or less at their present levels prior to the assumed ice age. In other words, the sea level would have dropped as the ice caps expanded, and then raised as the ice caps receded. Thus, there would have been a gradual change in sea level as the earth entered and then receded from the ice age. On the basis of this, the ice age theory as an explanation of the continental shelves does not seem acceptable, especially since these shelves are well defined, indicating that the sea level at one time, and for a long period of time, was at a point some 200 feet below present levels."

At this point Harry spoke up. "Reverend, I have heard that theory about the ice ages and their relation to the continental shelves, and always took it for granted that the scientists knew what they were talking about.

"However, as I was listening to your comments on this, it occurred to me that there is another strong argument against that theory. Since the present arctic regions were at one time subtropical or temperate in climate, there would not have been much, if any polar ice cap. In that case the ocean level would have been far higher than today, so how could the continental shelves have been the shoreline under those conditions? It seems rather obvious that the continental shelves must have represented the shoreline at some time, and since this could not have been at a time when there were no ice caps, when could it have been? According to the ice age theory, the sea level lowered during the expansion of the ice caps, and raised during the melting of the ice caps. This could not have produced a well defined shoreline represented by the continental shelves.

"Then too," Harry continued, "we now know that there are extensive fossil fuel deposits to be found under these continental shelves. Now, these must have resulted from accumulation of vast quantities of vegetation, and possibly animal life, to have been buried and converted into these fossil fuels. So, the continental shelves must have been out of the water for long periods of time for this to have taken place."

"That's a very fine observation," said Reverend Spangler, "and I agree with it entirely. Besides that, the very fact that some of these fossil fuel deposits are in areas that are now in the arctic zone, is evidence that there was little if any ice cap at the time these areas were *above* sea level. That is, during the very period during which the sea level would have been highest due to the absence of the ice caps, we find instead that these areas were in fact above sea level. Now, in all honesty, we must admit that in some areas there have been elevation of land masses, and in others, subsidence. Nevertheless, this can in no way explain the universal presence of continental shelves.

"Now, to get back to the ice comet theory that has been proposed by some to explain the flood, it is certainly possible that the addition of the water in such a case to that already on the earth would certainly have raised the level of the oceans by a considerable amount. This, plus the condensation of the dense atmospheric vapor, could then have inundated the low lying coastal plains, resulting in the continental shelves of today. Then the known process of elevation and subsidence would account for the varying depths at which these are found at the present time."

At this point Jim spoke up. "I must admit," he said, "that this is the first logical explanation I have ever heard concerning the continental shelves. In fact, when one stops to think about it, that is the only explanation of the flood and the continental shelves that makes sense. And, I can't see where it disagrees with the Scriptural account."

"Well, before we jump to conclusions and accept this theory as fact," Reverend Spangler said, "we must realize that this ice comet theory is just that. True, it makes sense, and does explain many things about both the flood and observed phenomena, such as the continental shelves and the frozen mammoths. However, there is not enough evidence from either science or Scripture to justify a dogmatic opinion on the subject. There is one thing that I am confident we can be dogmatic about, and that is the fact that the flood was an act of God. By no stretch of the imagination could Noah have foreseen the flood, assuming that this was a natural disaster. Now, as to the method God used or the extent of the flood, we cannot say with certainty. However, since it was an act of God, He certainly could have brought an ice comet into the picture to bring about the flood, or He could simply have temporarily set aside natural laws and caused the seas to leave their basins and cover the known world of that day. Frankly, on the basis of the description given in Scripture, I have a real problem in accepting the worldwide concept of the flood. Nevertheless, despite my reservations, I refuse to be dogmatic about it. Perhaps the flood was in fact worldwide, and we just do not have enough information to understand how it could be. One thing else I am sure about, and that is, that the sedimentary deposits found around the world on the highest mountains, are not evidence of the flood. In addition to the arguments I outlined earlier in our talks, there is another fact about these sedimentary deposits that disproves any claim that they were caused by the floods. I refer to footprints of pre-historic animals and birds, frequently found impressed in certain strata of the sedimentary rocks. Assuming that some animals had walked over newly deposited sediments as they were being formed by the rising waters, their footprints would have immediately been wiped out by the swirling water. This can be demonstrated very easily by walking on the beach near the edge of the water. Footprints are immediately wiped out by the incoming waves or tide. Frankly, it bothers me a great deal for religious leaders to use completely illogical and unsubstantiated ideas to prove a theory.

"It is my considered opinion that there can be only one true explanation of the events of creation, the length of days, the cause of the flood and its extent, and many other things that the Bible is not clear on. I also believe that when the answer is found, we will see complete harmony between Scripture and science."

There was quiet for a few moments after Reverend Spangler finished speaking. Then Jim said, "We have covered an awful lot of ground during the past several weeks. I wonder if you could give us a brief summary of what seems to be logical teaching of Scripture and some of the theories which tend to bring religion and science into harmony?"

"Well, I'll try," said Reverend Spangler. "First of all, astronomic and geologic observations and calculations show that the universe is running down, and therefore must have had a beginning. That there was such a beginning is confirmed by Scripture. Calculations indicate that this took place perhaps as much as seventeen billion years ago, at some point in space from which all of the galaxies, stars, and planets moved out into space. The Bible says that God spoke and they came into being, and by the breath of His mouth, all their host.

"Both science and Scripture agree that in its primeval, created form, the earth's surface was completely covered with water. It had no form and was devoid of life. The atmosphere, in my opinion, was carbon dioxide and nitrogen saturated with water vapor, so that no light of the sun penetrated to the surface. Then, the land mass separated from the water to produce a single continent. Now, whether we consider this as having resulted from the natural forces which God had initiated, or call it a Creative act, amounts to the same thing. Then, there came about a separation of the dense vapor covering the earth so that there was a clear air space between the earth's surface and the clouds above. With the earth prepared for life, God created vegetable life, followed by simple life forms, and then in stages, more and more advanced life forms, culminating with man. The vegetation thrived in the atmosphere containing carbode dioxide, and the lush vegetation provided a bountiful food supply for the animal life.

"In time, man multiplied on the earth, and some of these co-habited with either angelic beings or man-like creatures to pro-duce a race that became an abomination to God. To rid the world of these 'half-breeds,' God caused the flood, after warning Noah to build an ark for the protection of him and his family, along with pairs of all the animals designated as unclean and seven of those clean.

"At the designated time, God brought the flood upon the earth, most likely as a local flood to destroy the known world. Whether this resulted from the approach of an ice comet, or by some other miraculous event we can only speculate. But that God did it, we are sure. By the way, the advent of the rainbow would also confirm the opinion that there was a dense cloud cover prior to the flood, and that there had been no rain as we know it.

"There seems to be ample evidence, both Scriptural and sci-entific, to believe that the 'days' of Genesis were ages or eons, and it was during one of these that some great catastrophe caused huge masses of vegetation and animal life to be swept up, de-posited in low-lying areas and subsequently covered with sedi-ment. Gradually, these masses were compressed and changed to produce the fossil fuel deposits. In some areas, subsiding of the area caused a vast accumulation of sediment and even lime-stone, so that today it is not unusual to find crude oil at depths of five miles or more beneath the surface. In other areas, the accumulated vegetable and animal remains were not covered to any great extent, but became frozen to produce the tundra of Alaska and other Arctic regions.

"You will recall my mention of the asteroid belt, which is the name given to a large number of relatively small bodies of rock or metallic composition, traveling in an irregular orbit around the sun between Mars and Jupiter. There are some who believe that the catastrophic event that caused the destruction of the planet which is now represented by these fragments, also caused the tremendous upheavals, tidal waves and movement of continental plates which resulted in the destruction and burial of these vast amounts of vegetable and animal life on planet earth. During all of earth's history, changes have been taking place, such as volcanism, continental drift, elevation and subsidence of land masses, weathering, erosion, and chemical activity. These forces are still at work, continually changing the appearance and the environment of earth.

"The Bible and the geologic record both attest to the fact that the first life forms on earth were very simple, relatively speaking, but were followed by more and more complex forms, culminated by the more or less recent Creation of man. There were also changes taking place in the environment all during these eras, changes in weather patterns, and water and food supply. These changes resulted in mass movements of animal herds, and the necessity of adapting to these gradual changes in environment. As a result, changes took place in size, appearance and proportions of body parts. These changes are clearly visible today in animal life from one area, compared with similar species in other areas of the world. Even man is included, otherwise why would the people of one part of the world be so different in appearance from those in another part of the world? Just within the past generation, the average height of men in the U.S. has increased dramatically. However, despite these facts, it must be stressed that the changes that have occurred, whether in animal or man, were all in the area of adaptation, and not evolutionary. There is especially no evidence of transmutation, such as would be required to satisfy the Darwinian theory of evolution.

"The history of man is recorded in the Scriptures, and much of his more recent history is recorded in secular accounts. It is highly significant that secular history as well as archeology have confirmed, but never disproven, any of the Scriptural accounts, even though numerous efforts have been made to do so.[8, 9] Man appears to have inhabited the area of the Arabian peninsula between the Tigres and Euphrates rivers during the earliest times. It is highly doubtful that he had any idea of the size of the planet on which he lived. Thus, to him, the world was the inhabited world of that day. At least five thousand years ago, man had reached a civilized state in which he dwelt in cities, had developed many of the arts and cultures, and for the most part, had abandoned the worship of God, replacing it with idolatry and immorality. It was at such a time that Noah was forewarned by God of an impending cataclysm which would overtake the world. Thus warned, Noah embarked on the stupendous task of building a large boat so that he and his family, with the animals which God had commanded him to take, could be saved from the flood waters that were to come. The ark was finally completed, Noah was told to enter the ark with his family and the animals, and then the flood came. Nearly a full year passed before the waters returned from off the earth and Noah and his family, with the animals, were able to leave the ark, which had come to rest on Mt. Ararat. The continental shelves would seem to indicate that the sea level was raised perhaps 200 feet as a result of the flood, either as a result of the condensation of the heavy cloud layer, or from the residue of an ice comet, or from the melting of the polar ice caps.

"Now, I realize that many theologians will reject much of what I have been saying, since it appears to deny the miraculous. They will say that every aspect of creation, as well as the flood, were special acts of God, independent of natural forces. Now, there can be no question but that God has intervened in the history and even the private life of mankind. But this does not prove that every event recorded in Scripture was a special intervention, completely independent from natural forces. There is, in fact, ample evidence that God could and did use natural forces and the laws which He Himself had established, for special purposes.

"There must be a meeting place for those who believe in the Creation as being performed by God, and those who reject the Scripture. The Bible sets the stage. All of Creation, past and present, are the actors. The performance began in the dim ages past but is still going on. Like any story, we cannot fully understand the later part unless we are aware of the beginning, and have followed the plot. The theme is 'LOVE,' God's love for His special Creation, man, and His desire to share that love with intelligent, responsible individuals, who return that love by their own free choice. To accomplish this, He created the universe, prepared the earth, made life to come forth, and then Created man in His own image to have dominion over the earth He had prepared for him.

"Being finite Creatures of time, we tend to try to reduce the concept of the Creator to our level, and to place Him within the restrictions of time and space that we can understand. If we would but lift up our eyes, we would declare with the psalmist, 'The Heavens declare the glory of God, and the firmament showeth His handiwork.' "

CHAPTER XIII

Time

everal months had passed since Reverend Spangler and his two friends had had their last discussion on the subject of Creation. Their only contact since then was the usual casual meeting at church, so the good Reverend was just a little surprised when Harry Bolin came up to him at the close of the morning service one day and said, "Pastor, I just returned from a vacation with my family. We spent over a week up in the Rockies in Colorado, and while we were there, I paid special attention to the geologic formations and plant life. Several questions have come to mind as a result, and I wonder if I could come over some evening to discuss them with you?"

"Why, I'd be delighted to have you come," Reverend Spangler said. "How would this Friday be at, say, 7:00 o'clock?"

"That would be just fine," said Harry, and with that he took his leave.

Reverend Spangler was not at all surprised when Friday evening arrived to find that Harry Bolin had brought along their mutual friend and participant in former discussions, Jim Martin. After the usual greetings, the Reverend said, "Now, what did you find in the Rockies that proved so intriguing, Harry?"

"Well, mainly," he replied, "it was the rock formations. You recall when we were discussing some of the arguments concerning the flood, that you remarked about some of the theories which claim that the earth was relatively flat prior to the flood, and that for this reason, we find evidence of marine life scattered all over the earth, including high mountains. If that had been true, then the mountains as we see them today would have, of necessity, been raised to their present position during the period from the flood until now. I just don't see how that could be possible."

"Well, I agree with you that this does not seem possible," answered Reverend Spangler. "We know, from historical evidence as well as geologic evidence that there have been mountains much as we see them today for at least the last two or three thousands years. That would mean that the present mountains would have, of necessity, been raised prior to that time. The proponents of that theory claim that immediately after the flood, the present mountains were formed, and also that the waters of the flood receded down into the earth where they still are."

"I sure can't buy that theory," said Harry. "Scientists know that there is very little water deep under the surface of the earth, if for no other reason than that the temperature is too high for water to exist there. Even assuming that the earth was relatively flat at the time of the flood, which I don't accept either, the amount of water needed to cover the earth would have been hundreds, and perhaps thousands of times as much as can be accounted for under the surface of the earth."

"That's true," answered the Reverend, "and besides that, the Bible makes it unmistakenly clear that there were mountains before the flood. It states very plainly in the Genesis account that the waters covered the mountains *and the high mountains*. Even if the mountains were not as high as they are today, (and there is no evidence that that was true), the amount of water needed to cover even relatively low mountains would have been many times what can be accounted for in the earth. However,

96

another argument may be made to the effect that the oceans were not as deep at that time, and therefore the water collected in them after the flood. Here again, we must refer to the Biblical account which repeatedly refers to the fountains of the *deep*, surely suggesting that the oceans were known at that time to be deep.

"I believe this is one place we need to consult the Geologists and see what they have to say about the age of the mountains. According to Science, the earth began as a single continent located in the Antarctic. Then as a result of tremendous forces caused by currents in the underlying magma which makes up part of the outer layer of the earth's surface, this single continent broke up into several large 'plates' which gradually moved apart and eventually became the continents as we know them today. This is known as the tectonic plate theory. Even as we are sitting here, the plates making up the earth's surface are moving at known rates and in known directions. In some places the plates are moving apart, such as on the floor of the Pacific ocean. Extensive surveys have shown that one part is moving West, while another part is moving East. In between these plates, magma from deep in the earth is welling up to fill the void, causing a series of ripple-like ridges on either side. The speed at which these plates are separating has been determined quite accurately. It is also interesting to note that there is little if any sediment on the floor of the ocean close to the point of separation, but there is sediment in increasing depth as one moves out from this point, thus, showing that the movement has been going on progressively for a great length of time.

"Scientists have shown that the great earthquakes and volcanic activity around the world are primarily the result of the movement of these tectonic plates. Where two plates intersect, one tends to move under or against the other often causing it to become elevated, thus, building mountains. This is especially true on the west coast of the United States."

"Is that the reason for the sedimentary rocks found high in the Rockies?" asked Harry. "That is one of the things I noticed in particular. Even at 10,000 feet above sea level, many of the rocks were obviously sedimentary in nature."

"Yes, I am sure of that," answered the Reverend. "All of the evidence points to the fact that great areas of these United States were at one time below sea level. That is the reason we find fossils in these rocks. When the land was below sea level, sea life prevailed in those areas. Their fossilized remains were subsequently buried under sediment carried by the rivers and streams and thus preserved. Some were even converted into stone, and thus, the petrified fossils and vegetation, such as petrified wood, although the latter didn't grow under water of course. In every case, however, we find evidence that much of the land surface today was at one time much lower than today or, in other cases, dropped and was later elevated; that it was buried under sediment, ash or mud, and then at some later time was elevated and subjected to erosion, exposing many of the things we have just talked about to view.

"But, getting back to your comment about the extent and location of the vast sedimentary rocks, I think it is very important to recognize these for what they are, and how they came into existence. In order to have sedimentary rocks, there needs to be sediment, and sediment is the result of the gradual breakdown or erosion of rock. Now, we know that rocks do not suddenly decompose into small fragments the size of sand granules or even silt. This is a slow process brought about by the action of water, wind, frost, heat and attrition."

"What do you mean by attrition?" asked Jim, who until this moment had been a silent listener to the conversation. "Attrition is the act of rubbing together, such as happens in a fast moving stream, or as a result of waves pounding on a beach or against a rocky shoreline. If you have ever stopped along the West coast and observed the waves pounding against the rocks that, in some places, come right down to the ocean, you must realize that the rate at which these rocks are being eroded away is extremely slow. The point is, even a major flood with extremely violent waves, over a period of less than one year, would not have produced any substantial breakdown of the earth's surface. Therefore, the sediment which today makes up vast areas of the earth's surface, as loose sediment or soil and sand, or as sedimentary rock, must have been the result of tremendously long periods of gradual weathering and erosion of the primeval rock of which the earth was formed.

"In our earlier discussions I mentioned the uniformatarianism theory which some Creationists use as an argument against the theory of great age for the earth. I pointed out that the argument is directed toward the use by Science of a more or less uniform rate at which rocks disintegrate and sediments are formed. The creationists point out that under cataclysmic conditions, this rate may be many times the ordinary rate. While this is true and there may be some change in rate of disintegration of rock under severe conditions, the difference is nothing compared with the difference between the Science account of the earth's history and the 10,000-year age claimed by these Creationists. The rate would need to be at least 400,000 times as fast as at present for this to have been accomplished."

"But don't these same Creationists claim that God created the earth just as we see it today, and that these discrepancies were purposely created to confuse the wise?" asked Jim.

"Yes, some of them do take that position, but it is becoming more and more difficult for them to continue in that position," Reverend Spangler replied. "Even these individuals cannot deny the changes that are taking place right before their eyes. As a matter of fact, just within recent times, that is, the last couple of hundred years, coastlines have changed, new islands have been formed, landmarks have disappeared, and many minor changes have taken place. Just think of the vast amount of sediment and silt that rivers such as the Mississippi carry to the ocean each year. If this were to be multiplied by even the 10,000-year assumed age for the earth, it would show that the earth today is certainly not the same as it was at the time of Creation. The fact is, nothing remains the same, and there is no way we can honestly assume that the earth is the same today as it was at the time of Creation."

Now Harry spoke up again. "Isn't it true that the claims for a relatively young earth are an attempt to discredit the Evolutionary theory?"

"Yes, in part that is true," said Reverend Spangler. "However, in all honesty, we must also admit that many of these Creationists are convinced that the days of Creation, as set forth in the first chapter of Genesis, were in fact 24-hour days, and therefore, the earth cannot be more than about 10,000 years old."

"Is that the general feeling among Bible scholars and theologians?" asked Jim.

"No," replied the Reverend, "although up to a few years ago the vast majority of them did take that position. Much of this was the result of the translation of the original Hebrew and Greek texts into English, especially the King James version, where the word 'day' is used in the Genesis account. Of interest is the fact that newer translations have used the term 'eon' in place of 'day' in some cases, and according to the best sources, this is an acceptable alternative. However, I think one of the strongest arguments for the eon interpretation of the word usually translated 'day' is found in Genesis 2:4 & 5. You may recall that I referred to this in our earlier discussions. In these verses the word 'day' is used with regard to *all* of Creation, that is, everything included in the earlier six 'days.' For this reason, if no other, I am convinced that the word 'eon' is the proper translation. As I just mentioned, until a few years ago, most Bible scholars did accept the twenty-four hour day as the meaning of the word 'day' found in the King James translation. However, today, with the new translations plus all the geologic and astrologic evidence, many Bible scholars have changed their views on this subject. Of course, they still have the problem of Evolution to deal with. Fortunately, the Geologic evidence, and in particular the Geologic column, also confirms the account of Creation."

"How is that?" asked Jim.

"Well," Reverend Spangler replied, "science confirms the fact that the earliest life form recorded in the rocks was a very simple life form, which was followed by successively more and more complex life forms, culminating with man. This is exactly the order given in the Creation account. Perhaps of greatest significance, however, is the fact that Paleontologists have shown that new life forms generally appeared suddenly, rather than gradually and then increasing in numbers. Then of course, as I also mentioned earlier, there is no concrete evidence that a transmutation ever occurred. That is, one life form never changed to another, as for example fish to mammals or reptiles to birds. This is certainly understandable since if conditions were favorable for a particular form of life, why would it need to change; and if conditions were not favorable, it would not be able to survive. The Evolutionary theory proposed by Darwin requires tremendously long periods of time for any such change to take place. Significantly, conditions on the earth have not changed appreciably during all of earth's history since the first life form was created. In fact, life forms which existed hundreds of thousands of years ago still exist today. Why haven't they evolved?

"One of the most ridiculous theories I have ever heard concerns how man evolved from an ape-like creature. This theory suggests that these creatures spent so much time standing in water, searching for crustaceans, that they gradually lost their hair, and thus, man resulted. One wonders how this creature managed to retain hair on certain parts of the body by this practice, and especially how he managed to submerge everything but his eyebrows and his beard. Now I realize that I am being a little bit facetious by making that remark, but you will have to admit the theory is pretty far out. Seriously though, one must ask why the seals have not lost their hair, or muskrats, beaver, and other aquatic animals. What this boils down to, is that the Evolutionists have gone as far overboard in trying to substantiate their theories as the Creationists have in trying to refute Evolution.

"Very recently an article appeared in a Science magazine in which the author stated that more and more Scientists are rejecting the Darwinian Evolution theory, for the same reasons I spoke about earlier. However, they are not rejecting the concept of Evolution. Instead of the gradual, progressive evolution proposed by Darwin, they are suggesting a sort of instant change theory to explain the sudden appearance of new life forms as shown by Paleontology. These sudden changes are presumed to have occurred as a result of cataclysmic events and/or sudden environmental changes.

"Here again I would suggest that if there were rapid environmental changes that required physical changes in certain life forms in order to survive, they would have been exterminated before they could adapt. Furthermore, even changes brought about by adaptation to a changed environment would not have included transmutation."

At this point Harry glanced at his watch and immediately stood up and said, "Reverend, as usual this has been a very interesting and enlightening session. However, it is late and we must go. Could we meet again next week to continue our talks?"

"Why certainly," Reverend Spangler said. "How about the same time next week?"

"That's fine with me," said Jim.

"Me too," said Harry, "and thanks again for taking the time to talk to us. Good night."

CHAPTER XIV

Creation Summarized

t was a week later, and Harry Bolin and Jim Martin were once more seated in Reverend Spangler's living room. Harry began the discussion with a question. "Reverend, last week we were discussing the condition of the earth at the time of the flood. While I was up in the Rockies with my family, I also noticed that certain forms of vegetation grow only at certain elevations, especially trees. Now, how do those who claim that the earth was relatively flat prior to the flood account for the fact that certain trees are growing today at elevations of, say, 8,000 feet above sea level, but do not grow at lower elevations?"

"I know what you mean," Reverend Spangler replied. "I have noticed this same phenomenon myself. For instance, the aspens seem to grow only at about 7,000 to 9,000 feet above sea level. Therefore, if the earth had been relatively flat at the time of the flood, God must have created aspens at a later time, when there were high mountains. Of course, we don't accept this, and I believe that we have here additional proof that there were indeed high mountains prior to the flood, just as the Bible states. Actually, the number of individuals who hold to this particular theory is very small, and perhaps I shouldn't have spent so much time dealing with this theory.

"Speaking of time, I don't believe we ever gave any time to a discussion of that subject in our previous talks." "That's right, said Jim. "It seems to me that maybe this is the key to the whole matter."

"Well," said the Reverend, "I don't think I would go that far, but certainly time is something to be taken into account. I am not referring to time as related to years or the age of the earth, but rather time itself."

"Just what do you mean by that?" asked Harry.

"Well," continued the Reverend, "in the first place we must recognize that time is actually relative. Even the Bible makes that clear. Since we are discussing the Bible and spiritual matters, we should note two significant statements made in the Bible that, I think, are too often ignored or avoided as being beyond our understanding. The Bible makes the statement that 'A thousand years is as a day, and a day as a thousand years in God's sight.' Also, in the book of the Revelation the statement is made that 'time shall be no more.' Now, we believe that God is from everlasting to everlasting, that is, there is no beginning or end to His existence. I don't think we can comprehend this, being finite creatures. However, we do believe that God created all things, and I assume that by now we are all agreed that the earth is indeed very old in terms of years. Therefore, God must be older than even our universe. Yet, relatively, our universe has existed for but a moment as far as God is concerned. I think this is the only logical conclusion we may reach in view of the Scriptural statements that I just mentioned. You will remember too that I suggested that God and His universe are coexistent with ours, but so different that we have to consider them as a different dimension, not even based on the electromagnetic system which makes up our entire universe. If the make-up of this other dimension is so different, it is only logical to assume that time is also entirely different. We might think of this as a microbe looking at one of our days in comparison with the way a human would look at the same period of time. To the microbe a day would possibly be several generations, while to a human it is but a tiny fraction of a lifetime."

Reverend Spangler paused to let this thought sink in. There was silence for a few moments, then Jim spoke up. "I think I see what you are getting at, Reverend. What you are saying is that the millions or billions of years of the earth's existence, as far as man sees it, may be but a short time, (if we can use that expression), in God's sight."

"That's exactly what I mean," said the Reverend, "and I believe more and more theologians and Bible scholars are coming around to that understanding of time. In other words, as we look at our universe from God's perspective, a few billion years is not all that long. It seems to be human nature to want to bring God down to our level, or at least to place Him on our level."

"That certainly changes the whole picture as far as I am concerned," said Jim. "Looking at the matter from that point of view, it seems perfectly logical and reasonable that the original creation took place several billions of our years ago, yet, only briefly ago by God's standards. Then as the earth took shape according to laws which God had built into His creation, there came a time when life in the form of vegetation could flourish on the earth. As you mentioned earlier, the primeval atmosphere most certainly consisted of carbon dioxide and nitrogen primarily. No other gaseous mixture would have supported vegetation, and obviously vegetation had to precede animal life, since animal life is totally dependent on vegetable life for existence. Also, since vegetation gives off oxygen as it converts carbon dioxide into plant material, there came a time when the atmosphere was suitable for animal life. It was then that God began His creative acts starting with simple life forms, and then with more and more complex forms, just as the book of Genesis recounts, and just as the Geologists find recorded in the fossils of the earth. And all of this in a brief time as God sees it, but over eons as man sees it.

"Thus all seems so simple, yet, so grandiose. I think in the pride of our intellect, man has choked on a gnat while swallowing a camel, as the Scripture puts it."

"I couldn't have expressed it better," said Reverend Spangler. "I agree," added Harry, "and as far as I am concerned, that settles the whole matter for me. At last it all makes sense and as you have said, Reverend, the Bible appears to support this in many cases, and in no case is there any contradiction. I really appreciate this chance to talk to you again Pastor, and I trust that we have not taken too much of your time. I'm ready to go now. How about you, Jim?" "Yes, I'm ready too, Harry. Pastor, I'd like to add my thanks to Harry's. It has been very encouraging and enlightening to discuss these matters with you again." With these words of thanks, both men left the house, leaving the good Reverend to sit quietly for a time meditating over the conversations he had just concluded. "Wouldn't it be wonderful," he said to himself, "if Christians everywhere could all accept the simple straightforward resumé that Jim had presented. Then instead of arguing with each other over the length of the days of creation or the extent of the flood or the condition of the earth prior to the flood, they could unite behind a solid front to refute the claims of the Evolutionists, and give God the glory for the great things He has done." With a sigh of resignation, realizing that this would probably never take place, he turned off the lights and retired for the night.

The End

INDEX

References:

1. Science & Creation Handbook for Teachers.
2. Family Circle, April 1972, p. 18.
3. Earth's Earliest Ages—Pember.
4. Exodus, Chapter 20, Verse 11.
5. National Geographic Vol. 141, No. 5, p. 585.
6. Paleontology—Berry
7. Steeg—Radio Message RMO 12 p. 3.
8. Archeology and The Bible—Owens.
9. Paleontology—Berry.

SPECIAL NOTE: You may order a copy of this book for yourself, or as a gift for a friend, directly from:

Ralph Tanner Associates, Inc.
122 North Cortez Street
Prescott, Arizona 86301

Please enclose check or money order for $12.50 plus $2.50 for packaging/postage. Arizona residents only, add 6% sales tax.